D0930151

Sex Discrimination in Career Counseling and Education

Michele Harway
Helen S. Astin

Published in cooperation with the Higher Education Research Institute, Inc., Los Angeles, California

The Praeger Special Studies program—utilizing the most modern and efficient book production techniques and a selective worldwide distribution network—makes available to the academic, government, and business communities significant, timely research in U.S. and international economic, social, and political development.

Sex Discrimination in Career Counseling and Education

PRAEGER SPECIAL STUDIES IN U.S. ECONOMIC, SOCIAL, AND POLITICAL ISSUES

780676

Praeger Publishers New York London

Library of Congress Cataloging in Publication Data

Harway, Michele, 1947–
  Sex discrimination in career counseling and
education.

  (Praeger special studies in U.S. economic,
social, and political issues)
  Includes bibliographical references.
  1.   Personnel service in education—United
States.   2.   Sex discrimination—United States.
3.   Vocational guidance—United States.   I.   Astin,
Helen S., 1932–   joint author.   II.   Title.
LB1027.5.H355   373.1'4'0973   77-7829
ISBN 0-03-021826-8

This research was done under contract No. 300-75-0206 and No. 300-75-2027 with the Education Division. Contractors undertaking projects with government sponsorship are encouraged to express freely their professional judgment. Points of view or opinions, therefore, do not necessarily represent positions or policies of the Education Division, and no official endorsement should be inferred.

National Center for Education Statistics
Education Division
U.S. Department of Health, Education, and Welfare

PRAEGER SPECIAL STUDIES
200 Park Avenue, New York, N.Y., 10017, U.S.A.

Published in the United States of America in 1977
by Praeger Publishers,
A Division of Holt, Rinehart and Winston, CBS, Inc.

789   038   987654321

PREFACE

The Women's Educational Equity Act of 1974, which constitutes Section 408 of the Education Amendments of 1972, proposes to provide educational equity for women in the United States. Section 408 (f) (4) states:

> From the sums available for the purposes of this section, the Commissioner is authorized and directed to conduct a national, comprehensive review of sex discrimination in education, to be submitted to the Council not later than a year after the date of enactment of this section. The Council shall review the report of the Commissioner and shall make recommendations, including recommendations for additional legislation, as it deems advisable.

This book presents the results of research done under contracts awarded to the authors in compliance with the Women's Educational Equity Act. Reports on the contracts were entitled "Sex Discrimination in Guidance and Counseling" by Michele Harway, Helen S. Astin, Jeanne M. Suhr, and John M. Whiteley, and "Sex Discrimination in Access to Postsecondary Education" by Helen S. Astin, Michele Harway, and Patricia McNamara. In this book, we focus primarily on vocational counseling and participation in postsecondary education. Following a review of existing research and literature and a critical discussion of the knowledge in this area, the book presents implications for policy and modes to implement needed changes.

This study had the support, advice, and assistance of many persons. We would like to acknowledge the assistance of C. E. Christian and James Henson, research analysts at the Higher Education Research Institute (HERI). Ms. Christian and Mr. Henson conducted the computer analyses for the exploratory studies. In addition, Ms. Christian conducted one exploratory survey in the Los Angeles metropolitan-area high schools and analyzed the data. Patricia McNamara, Jeanne M. Suhr, and John M. Whiteley were integrally involved in the project from the beginning and wrote portions of the report from which this book is derived. Lewis C. Solmon, executive officer of HERI, provided much support and assistance throughout the project.

Four consultants provided expertise on different aspects of the study. Lorenza Schmidt and Marguerite Archie were most helpful in sensitizing us to issues of minorities. Wendy Williams, a lawyer with Equal Rights Advocates, a public-interest law firm, helped us examine findings in the context of recent legislation. Arthur J. Lange gave us important information on assertion training. Another consultant, Rita M. Whiteley, contributed the ideas on feminist counseling and assertion training and wrote a draft for the earlier report.

v

Alexander W. Astin read the manuscript, offering numerous insights and suggestions.

We would like to thank Sally Anderson, Carol Feldman, Kathleen Kaufman, Valerie Kesler, and Mary Ruth Swint, who typed and retyped the many drafts. Beverly T. Watkins edited the manuscript.

CONTENTS

LIST OF TABLES AND FIGURES

LIST OF ABBREVIATIONS

ASS	Affirmative action statements
AAUW	American Association of University Women
ACE	American Council on Education
ACT	American College Testing Program
ACES	Association for Counselor Education and Supervision
AHED	Association for Humanistic Education and Development
AMEG	Association for Measurement and Evaluation in Guidance
ANC	Association for Nonwhite Concerns
APA	American Psychological Association
APGA	American Personnel and Guidance Association
BEOG	Basic Educational Opportunity Grant
CCHE	Carnegie Commission on Higher Education
CEEB	College Entrance Examination Board
CEW	Continuing education for women
CIJE	Current Index to Journals in Education
CIRP	Cooperative Institutional Research Program
CPC	College Placement Center
ECVG	*Encyclopedia of Careers and Vocational Guidance*
ERIC	Education Resource Information Center
GSL	Guaranteed Student Loan
HEGIS	Higher Education General Institution Surveys
HERI	Higher Education Research Institute
KOIS	Kuder Occupational Interest Survey
NASP	National Association of School Psychologists
NCES	National Center for Educational Statistics
NCGC	National Catholic Guidance Conference
NDEA	National Defense Education Act
NDSL	National Direct Student Loan
NEA	National Education Association
NIE	National Institute of Education
NIH	National Institutes of Health
NLS	National Longitudinal Study
NSSFNS	National Scholarship Service and Fund for Negro Students
NSVCS	Non-Sexist Vocational Card Sort
NVGA	National Vocational Guidance Association
OOH	*Occupational Outlook Handbook*
RIE	Research in Education
SAT	Scholastic Achievement Test
SCII	Strong-Campbell Interest Inventory
SDS	Self-Directed Search
SEGO	Sex Equality and Guidance Opportunities
SES	Socioeconomic status

x

SIF   Student Information Form
SVIB   Strong Vocational Interest Blank
TFSWP   Task Force on the Status of Women in Psychology

Sex Discrimination in Career Counseling and Education

CHAPTER

1

INTRODUCTION

What do we mean by sex discrimination in counseling? One objective of counseling is to expose students to all possible goals. Conversely, sex bias in counseling is "that condition or provision which influences a person to limit his or her considerations of career opportunities solely on the basis of that person's sex" (AMEG, 1973, p. 172). To expand the definition, sex bias in counseling is any condition under which a client's options are limited by the counselor solely because of gender. That would include limiting expression of certain kinds of behavior because they have not traditionally been appropriate for one sex. Sex bias in counseling may be overt: for example, suggesting that a female high school student not enroll in a math class because "women aren't good in math," thereby limiting her later options to enter scientific or professional careers. Or it may be covert: subtle expectations or attitudes that "girls always are" certain stereotypic characteristics.

Since inequities in the treatment of women can begin at birth and continue through life—at home, in school, in society at large—even if equal counseling treatment were provided to students independent of sex, one would expect different outcomes. It seems obvious that equal treatment of people with different experiences would merely maintain the difference in opportunities for men and women. Equity for members of each sex will probably require differential treatment by sex, rather than equal treatment for all. While the counselor's role has traditionally been to explore options with students passively, counselors will need to encourage women actively to seek nontraditional careers because their socialization may prompt them to consider only the most traditional. Counselors will have to make special efforts to ensure that young women become all they can be, rather than develop along stereotypic lines. Equity should be achieved by affirmative action—not by passive approval or disapproval of a student's choice, but by an active affirmative step to enhance the student's

1

options. Moreover, the traditional linkage of stereotypic characteristics with sex, the resultant discrimination, and the contrast with the realities of everyday life (such as child care) generate ambiguity for many women who become uncertain of their sex roles. The role of the counselor, then, involves exploring with the female client her role ambiguity and her options.

Counseling assumes an interactive process between two or more individuals in which the attitudes and prior experiences of both affect the outcome. It is not a one-time event in which the counselor provides information to the student. The counseling interaction may consist of one or more sessions over short or long periods, and its effects may last beyond the conclusion of the interaction.

While counseling is often thought to mean secondary school counseling, this study considers counseling as it affects individuals at different stages of development. Figure 1, which illustrates the interaction between student variables and counseling interventions, indicates that concerns other than counseling may, singly or in combination with counseling, affect the outcome; that is, background, race, sex, and socioeconomic status (SES) will account for the socialization of the student. These factors may affect motivation and self-esteem, determining whether the student pursues postsecondary education and which program he/she chooses.

If the student makes a certain choice about his/her future educational plans, that choice may not be due to a counselor's discriminatory intervention but to the student's socialization or socioeconomic stratum. Thus, to examine only counselor-student interaction and to conclude from that interaction or its consequence that the counselor is discriminating is simplistic.

The dyadic counseling process (Figure 2), the main focus of the study, can be compared with a chemical process in that two major ingredients, student characteristics and counselor characteristics, interact to form a counseling interaction. While the characteristics (for example, background, race, expectations) of the two participants are not themselves viewed as discriminatory, they give the observer a baseline. In determining whether discrimination has occurred during the counseling process, an observer can only understand the process by considering the counseling outcomes and the characteristics of both participants.

SCOPE OF THE STUDY

An overview of the effects of the educational system and society on the student is presented in Chapter 2. To understand the impact of guidance and counseling, it is necessary to understand the characteristics the individual brings to the situation. C. F. Cannell and R. L. Kahn (1968) argue that

each person somes to the interview with many fixed attitudes, personality characteristics, and stereotypes of other groups. Both

FIGURE 1

Relationship of Background Variables, Counseling, and Outcomes

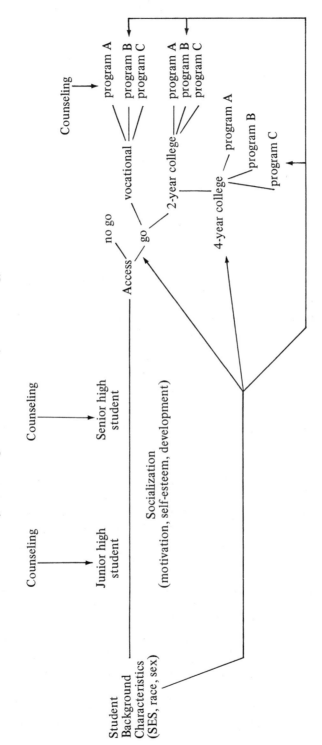

Source: M. Harway, H. S. Astin, J. M. Suhr, and J. M. Whiteley, "Sex Discrimination in Guidance and Counseling," report for the National Center for Educational Statistics, U.S. Department of Health, Education, and Welfare (Washington, D.C.: Government Printing Office, 1976).

FIGURE 2

Dyadic Counseling Process

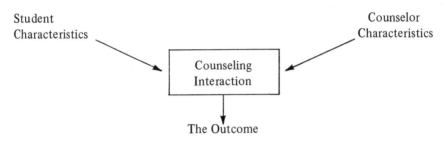

Source: M. Harway, H. S. Astin, J. M. Suhr, and J. M. Whiteley, "Sex Discrimination in Guidance and Counseling," report for the National Center for Educational Statistics, U.S. Department of Health, Education, and Welfare (Washington, D.C.: Government Printing Office, 1976).

respondent and interviewer also possess characteristics visible to the other and suggestive of group membership and group identifications—age, sex, race, religious background, income, and educational status (p. 549).

They cite two ways in which background characteristics may affect the interview process: (1) They may play a part in determining the psychological characteristics of both parties, including the relevant perceptions, attitudes, and motives. If the two persons are from widely different backgrounds, mutual understanding may be more difficult. (2) Background characteristics provide one participant with cues about the other. For example, if the student is assigned to a counselor of another race, this difference may affect his/her attitude or behavior toward the counselor and, consequently, the results of the counseling interaction itself. The student's sex or race may in turn lead the counselor to certain expectations about the counselee's ability, motivation, and achievement orientation.

The purpose of Chapter 2 is not to document instances of discrimination but to contribute to understanding the forces that have impacted on the student prior to his/her first experience with a secondary school counselor. These characteristics are a function of the individual's previous experience with parents, school, and media.

The educational system has been identified by several writers as dealing unequally with the two sexes (Harrison, 1973; Frazier and Sadker, 1973; MacLeod and Silverman, 1973). In a sense, the educational system mirrors society: In a society that deals unequally with men and women, the schools will deal unequally with boys and girls. The first part of Chapter 2 provides evidence from developmental data on sex differences (Maccoby and Jacklin, 1974), from reports documenting harmful effects of teacher expectation (Rosenthal and Jacobson, 1968), and from the media on the part they play in conveying sex roles. The impact of family and friends on future plans of the child through high school is also examined.

The last part of Chapter 2 documents the development of other student characteristics that can affect guidance experiences. Motivation, self-concept, and the attitudes of students toward women, especially women and work, affect the likelihood that the student will seek nontraditional alternatives on his/her own.

Many social myths about achievement, motivation, self-concept, and women's place in society persist. While acceptance of women working seems to be increasing, career options are restricted largely to traditionally feminine areas. Women believe that the ideal woman should strive for a balance between self-realization and intrafamily nurturing. But women's view of men's ideal woman is significantly more family oriented and personally subordinated. This belief inhibits some women from seeking work because they believe that men prefer traditional homemakers. Moreover, success and achievement are considered masculine attributes. When a woman is successful, either the quality of her achievement is devalued or a multitude of negative consequences is associated with her success. Since success by women is not highly valued even by other women, for women to seek success requires high self-motivation and an internalized reward system.

Chapter 3 examines the participation of women in educational activity. The first part of the chapter ascertains the extent to which women are taking advantage of all available educational opportunities, since the kind and amount of education have implications for their future occupational opportunities.

Counselors are needed to assist women to prepare adequately while in high school and to provide them with information for postsecondary decisions. Thus, before a discussion of the counselors and their role and how information provided by counselors and counseling materials affects women, the participation of women in high school courses and programs must be examined. This chapter analyzes the issues of access and choice of postsecondary education. Expressed occupational interests of young women are also examined, since such information is critical for counselors as they assist young women during the developmental years with their educational and occupational decisions.

The chapter concludes with the implication for counseling and socialization's effect on the educational achievement of women.

Chapter 4 looks at counselor training and the composition of the counseling profession to determine which background variables might affect guidance. Racial and sexual breakdowns of the membership of several counselor professional groups are presented in this chapter. Moreover, the chapter includes an examination of counselor education programs including courses and textbooks.

Chapter 5 discusses the counseling process. The first part of the chapter concentrates on the effect of race and sex on counseling and counselor. Most studies show that the experiences of the counselor and the human qualities of both counselor and client, rather than counselor-client race and sex similarity, are the important dimensions. Research on counselor attitudes is highly complex. While data indicate that most mental health professionals hold negative or ambivalent attitudes toward women, delineation of the impact of these attitudes on the counseling interaction requires further research.

The second part of Chapter 5 assesses counseling instruments and materials, including college and proprietary school catalogs, for sex bias. Tests and test manuals, illustrations in career materials, and the content and illustrations in catalogs reflect sex-role stereotypes.

Chapter 6 examines the few data available on counseling outcomes, studying the impact of different types of counseling. Conclusive results are scarce; much more research is needed.

Novel approaches to counseling women, ranging from those developed and applied in traditional settings to those out of the mainstream that show promise, are presented in Chapter 7, which describes the problems and evaluates new approaches. Findings attest to the great wealth of recent developments.

Chapter 8 ties the data together to present some conclusions and implications for four groups: legislators, researchers, institutions, and counselors.

METHOD AND PROCEDURES

Hypotheses were formulated for seven areas of inquiry vital to sex discrimination in guidance and counseling:

Socialization, which plays an important role in shaping the educational and career decisions of young people, reflects the sex-role biases of the surrounding society.

Socialization affects women's achievement motivation, an effect that results in their limited participation in educational activity unless it is counteracted by good counseling.

The counselor training field reflects the biases and sex-role stereotypes of the larger society.

Counselor trainers and training rationales may reinforce existing biases or produce attitudes and values that interfere with equitable counseling practices.

Tests (personality, interest) and other source materials used to assess clients and assist them with their educational, vocational, and personal decisions reflect sex-role biases.

Negative outcomes of counseling, reflected in students' educational and career decisions, indicate acceptance of sex-role stereotypes.

Existing counseling programs can be freed of sex biases through implementing new approaches in counselor training and procedures.

The critical analysis used in this research depends heavily on three data sources:

1. Existing research and theoretical literature.
2. Reexamination and presentation of data from statistical sources, for example, Project TALENT (see Appendix); U.S. Bureau of the Census; National Center for Educational Statistics (NCES); and the Cooperative Institutional Research Program (CIRP; see Appendix).
3. Exploratory studies that address questions for which information is lacking in either the theoretical and research literature or the statistical profiles of high school and college youth (see details in Appendix).

CHAPTER

2

SOCIALIZATION

Socialization refers to the pattern of antecedent variables that shape behavior and tie it to the social system in which an individual lives (Hess, 1970). It is step-by-step learning of behavior appropriate to one's role in society. Of primary concern is the process by which children learn to be men and women. The importance of early socialization in determining behavior, perceptions, and preferences in high school and beyond makes it imperative that this process be explored for potential sex bias that would incline a person to limit his/her own options or those of another individual. Both external factors (the school system, the media, and parental behavior) and internal mechanisms (self-concept, achievement motivation, and sex-role stereotypes) contribute to socialization and counteract change.

To explore the contribution of various socialization mechanisms, it is important to look at the differences in behavior that exist between the sexes. Sex differences may exist in emotional reactions to people and events, in the vigor with which men and women attack life's problems, and in the potential for acquiring knowledge and skills for occupations (Maccoby and Jacklin, 1974). What are these behaviors and what are the advantages or limitations of differences for the individual? If psychological sex differences do exist, how do they come about? Are they inevitable (behavioral tendencies) or products of arbitrary social stereotypes? Do they impose limitations or expectations on the lives of each sex (Maccoby and Jacklin, 1974)?

In their critical summary of empirical evidence of sex differences, E. E. Maccoby and C. N. Jacklin concluded that while some sex differences are quite well established, others are myths, and still others require additional evidence before their reliability can be ascertained.

Some established sex differences appear in verbal, visual-spatial, and mathematical abilities. While boys and girls tend to be nearly equal in these

8

abilities until early adolescence, in the early teens girls tend to surpass boys in verbal ability and boys to surpass girls in visual-spatial and mathematical abilities. Another difference is in aggression. As early as age two, boys appear more aggressive than girls. This finding tends to be consistent cross-culturally.

Maccoby and Jacklin identified numerous alleged sex differences that, in light of empirical data, have proved to be unfounded beliefs. "Beginning in infancy, the two sexes show a remarkable degree of similarity in the basic intellectual process of perception, learning, and memory. . . . The allegation that girls learn best by rote processes, boys by some more advanced form of reasoning is clearly not supported by evidence" (pp. 61-62). Other unfounded beliefs are that girls are more "social" and "suggestible" than boys, that girls have lower self-esteem and lack achievement motivation, that boys are more analytical, that girls are more affected by heredity and boys by environment, and that girls are auditory and boys visual.

Girls do rate themselves higher in social competence. Boys often see themselves as strong, powerful, dominant, and "potent." Boys' achievement motivation appears more responsive to competitive arousal than that of girls, but this does not imply that it is higher. During college (but not earlier or later) men have a greater sense of control over their own fate and greater confidence in their probable performance on a variety of college tasks. Research on sex difference in tactile sensitivity, fear, timidity and anxiety, activity, competitiveness, dominance, compliance, and nurturance has yielded inconsistent results and requires further exploration (Maccoby and Jacklin, 1974).

Longitudinal studies reviewed by M. B. Cohen (1966) showed that boys who are most active in childhood become strongly masculine and sexually active, but weaker in intellectual striving in adulthood. The same study suggested that boys nurtured by their mothers give up passivity and dependency under societal pressure in adulthood, but replace these behavior characteristics with social anxiety, sedentary and intellectual careers, and low levels of sexual activity. Cultural pressures on girls to be traditionally feminine cause withdrawal from challenging tasks and decreasing interest in intellectual development. Inborn tendencies toward activity and passivity in boys and girls are not reversed but repressed, resulting in anxieties about not being appropriately masculine or feminine (Cohen, 1966). This finding suggests that activity and passivity may not be naturally sex-typed behaviors but become so through cultural conditioning.

Empirically supported behavioral sex differences do not appear to constitute sufficient reasons for differences in male and female roles. A child learns early which behaviors and characteristics are appropriate for males and females. By age two and one-half, children are already able not only to distinguish males from females but also to sort correctly into piles utensils and clothing used by the two sexes—screwdrivers for "daddies" and aprons for "mommies" (Vener and Snyder, 1966).

At least two processes are at work in the evolution of these perceptions: learning of appropriate sex-typed behaviors and learning of cultural sex-role stereotypes. Sex-types behaviors refer to "role behavior appropriate to a child's ascribed gender" (Maccoby and Jacklin, 1974, p. 177). Sex typing deals with establishing a pattern of "feminine" or "masculine" interests and activities. Maccoby and Jacklin found that parents encourage their children to develop sex-typed interests or provide them sex-typed toys. More strongly, they discourage their children, especially their sons, from inappropriate sex-typed behaviors and activities.

In their study of kindergarten and sixth-grade students, N. K. Schlossberg and J. Goodman (1972a) found that these children, regardless of age, can identify traditionally masculine and feminine occupations. In addition, these children choose occupations that fall within the usual stereotypes. A study of fifth graders revealed similar results. Boys and girls demonstrated sex-stereotypic perceptions of occupations and personality traits. Although girls are less willing to reverse traditional sex-tied jobs, they are more willing to see occupations open to either sex. Further, girls have varied career aspirations: Only 6 percent would be only a mother or housewife. There is, however, a marked discrepancy between the stated career goal and the way girls would spend a day in the future. They focus on marriage and family, while boys focus on career and job (Iglitzen, 1973). While a girl at this age may plan for a career, other elements of socialization have not provided her with a picture of what would be involved in her role as a career person. The adult women she sees focus on marriage and family; this is the adult female role with which she is most familiar.

Children see certain jobs and traits as masculine and feminine. These perceptions have implications for level of aspiration and self-esteem. For example, the U.S. Department of Labor Women's Bureau (1972) has published data on women's participation in the work force. It is well documented that traditionally female jobs are lower paying than traditionally male jobs, and hence lower in status. A small fraction of professional positions—doctors, engineers, college professors—are filled by women. The lowest-status jobs also have small percentages of women participants. Women hold an overwhelming majority of middle-level clerical jobs. The median income of women, within a given occupational grouping, is only 50 percent to 60 percent that of men. Starting salaries, when two applicants have the same qualifications but differ in sex, show a similar discriminatory pattern.

PARENTAL BEHAVIOR, THE EDUCATIONAL SYSTEM, AND SOCIETY

The sex-typing of behaviors and the accompanying sex-role stereotypes described above inhibit self-understanding. In contrast, counseling seeks to optimize an individual's choices through self-understanding. Thus, a student may bring into counseling sex-role stereotypes that may limit his/her ability to consider the variety of career options.

How does a child learn those culturally conditioned sex-typed behaviors? Through the many agents of socialization—parents, peers, television, teachers, and others. Counseling and guidance personnel and materials are only two among the many. To maintain a perspective on the potential impact of guidance and counseling, it is necessary to consider the effect of these other agents before and during school.

Sex ascription begins at birth when a baby is tagged male or female (the first bit of information parents learn about this new individual). The impact of this knowledge on parental behavior is, however, unclear. There do exist a large number of studies (Bing, 1963; Crandall et al., 1964; Shaw and White, 1965; Heilbrun, 1969) and literature reviews (Zigler and Child, 1968; Mischel, 1970; Maccoby and Jacklin, 1974) that explore the relationship between parental attitudes and practices and child development. M. Lewis (1972) suggested that from the first contact parents deal differently with male and female children. They caress and speak softly to girls and throw their boys into the air more. Later they interact verbally more frequently with their girls. Maccoby and Jacklin, in their review of differential socialization of the sexes, concluded that while parents do not appear to prepare their children differently for adult sexual "double standards," parents actively encourage sex-typed interests, provide children with sex-typed toys, and actively discourage behavior considered inappropriate for that sex. Boys seem somewhat more restricted; they are punished more but probably also receive more praise and encouragement. Adults respond as though they find boys more interesting or attention-provoking than girls. Boys appear to have a more intense socialization experience, which undoubtedly has consequences for their development, including their values and future activities.

In addition to family influences, children's literature and television are major information sources available for processing by preschool children. Of course, television and other mass media continue to be major socializing influences throughout an individual's life.

A content analysis of a large number of children's books revealed that women are grossly underrepresented. Where they appear, traditional sex-role stereotypes are reinforced: Boys are active, girls are passive; boys lead and rescue, girls follow and serve others. Adult men and women are also sex typed: Men engage in a wide variety of occupations, women are wives and mothers (Weitzman et al., 1972).

Analyses of elementary, high school, and college textbooks indicated similar biases. Protagonists in stories tend to be male; girls are portrayed as helpers and watchers, not doers; they are described as timid, helpless, and dependent. The occupations follow rigid, traditional sex lines: women are teachers, nurses;

men are firemen, doctors, policemen (Women on Words and Images, 1972). In J. S. MacLeod and S. T. Silverman's (1973) analysis of major government textbooks, a misrepresentation or lack of representation is accorded women. They are virtually excluded as historical figures and from descriptions and illustrations. When they are included, women are objects of derision in cartoons or they are in subordinate and supportive rather than leadership roles.

At least the message is consistent: Girls and women are sociable, kind, and timid, but inactive, unambitious, and uncreative. Boys and men are active, aggressive, tough, and successful. If these books are typical of other social influences, it is small wonder girls develop an inferiority complex about their sex (MacLeod and Silverman, 1973).

Another, perhaps subtler, area is language. Schneider and Hacker (1973) documented the effect of the generic term "man" in textbooks at the college level. Among college students, "man" is usually interpreted as "male" rather than as "male and female." In high school government textbooks the use of masculine terminology implies exclusion of women (MacLeod and Silverman, 1973). If this is the perception of relatively sophisticated college and high school students, is it not more likely to affect younger children to a greater degree? Are they not likely, upon hearing "mankind" and masculine pronouns used repeatedly, to believe that women are nonexistent or at least unimportant? H. A. Bosmajian (1972), presenting the impact language has on identity, noted that language has been used to maintain inequities, injustices, and subjugation.

Visual mass media are another socializing influence at the preschool level and later. One review (Women on Words and Images, 1975) showed that frequent television viewing begins for most children at age three and remains high until age twelve (Schramm, Lyle, and Parker, 1961; Lyle and Hoffman, 1972). Children sometimes model their own behavior after behavior observed on television, and some generalization of behavior does take place (Liebert, Neale, and Davidson, 1973; Friedrich and Stein, 1973). In fact, audiovisual modeling is used to help children overcome phobias and withdrawal symptoms (Bandura, Ross, and Ross, 1961; Liebert, Neale, and Davidson, 1973). If children attend closely to messages on television, the program content becomes crucial. Women on Words and Images (1975) has completed an analysis of sex stereotyping showing that prime-time television communicates the message that there are more men around and that they are dominant, authoritative, and competent. While neither sex displays a majority of positive behaviors, women show more negative behaviors than men:

> Archie [Bunker] may be mean-spirited but he is dominant and authoritatively mean, a master of the put-down as well. Edith is incompetent, dependent, and a victim. The few times when she does successfully solve a problem, she belittles herself. Together, they serve as models of adult life in contemporary America for children

who sit in front of their television sets, laughing along with the sound track at the way men and women get along (p. 30).

"The greater power of the male to control his own destiny is part of the cultural stereotype of maleness and is embedded in images on television and in print. Women could be externalizers by reason of cultural shaping alone" (Maccoby and Jacklin, 1974, p. 157). Given the written and visual message women receive, it is not surprising that studies on how women perceive themselves, how they believe they are perceived by men, and how men perceive them suggest sharp contrasts and inconsistencies that would produce conflicts in women and communication problems between the sexes (Astin, Suniewick, and Dweck, 1974).

If a child should reach elementary school without being thoroughly exposed to sex-role stereotypes, this condition will be counteracted by the sexism that pervades schools (McCandless, 1969; Bernstein, 1972; Weitzman et al., 1972; Women on Words and Images, 1972; Frazier and Sadker, 1973; Levy, 1973; Saario, Jacklin, and Tittle, 1973; Harrison, 1973). Aside from the obvious stereotyping in textbooks, other more covert instances of sexism may occur in the classroom. The teacher may allow different kinds of behavior by the two sexes or may utilize his or her own different disciplinary practices for boys and girls. Many studies have addressed the issue of female teachers' discrimination against boys. The results, however, indicate that boys in general, far from being discriminated against, receive more positive as well as negative attention, more praise, more instruction, and more encouragement to be creative (Sears and Feldman, 1966). The school's "feminization" or "domestication" training is seen as good preparation for "real womanhood." In fact, girls are doubly trained at home and at school to be docile and conforming (Levy, 1973). It is not unwarranted to suppose that such differential training will lead to different levels of achievement and self-concept (Sears and Feldman, 1966).

As early as kindergarten, curriculum and activities may be different for each sex. Both sexes may not have equal access to all play materials: Girls may be directed toward housekeeping areas equipped with dolls and toy stoves, while boys may be encouraged to play ball or build with blocks. Teachers may compound the situation by using stereotypic bulletin board materials, for example, a display called "Men at Work" showing individuals in traditional sex-role occupations only. Having boys empty wastebaskets and girls dust is another example of possible sexist practices of teachers. Reviews of research and educational materials (books, tests) and curriculums and practices in elementary schools (McCandless, 1969; Bernstein, 1972; Levy, 1973; Saario, Jacklin, and Tittle, 1973) indicate that the structure and content of the American school system contribute to sex-role stereotyping and discriminate against both male and female students, limiting children's experiences.

How can one be sure that sex-role stereotyping affects children? R. Rosenthal and L. Jacobson (1968) documented the impact of the self-fulfilling prophecy in the educational context. While the study has subsequently been criticized for its methodology, it does parallel other studies of the self-fulfilling prophecy but puts the concept in an educational context. Basically, the idea of the self-fulfilling prophecy is that one person's prophecy of another's performance can determine that performance. In an empirical test, Rosenthal and Jacobson pretested all children enrolled in one school with a standard nonverbal intelligence test represented to teachers as one that would predict intellectual "blooming" or "spurting." About 20 percent of the children were later alleged to be potential spurters. Teachers were given the names of the alleged spurters, who were actually chosen at random. The difference between the "special" and the "ordinary" child then was only in the mind of the teacher. All children were retested at three later times and their gains in IQ computed between the different testing periods. After the first year a significant expectancy advantage appeared; that is, 47 percent of the special children or "bloomers" gained 20 or more IQ points compared with only 19 percent of the control children. In addition, bloomers were rated more intellectually curious, happier, and less in need of social approval by their teachers.

How did such changes occur? Rosenthal and Jacobson suggested that the teacher may have communicated subliminally to the "special" children that he/she expected improved performance. Such communication, plus changes in teaching techniques, may have helped the child learn by changing his/her self-concept, motivation, and expectations of behavior, as well as cognitive styles and skills. Similarly, teacher expectations that a girl will be passive and docile, with high verbal but low quantitative ability, may result in the child's displaying those characteristics.

The school authority structure (male principals, female teachers) clearly teaches students the differential status, as do segregated classes and activities (Levy, 1973). It is rare that a child sees a man playing the loving, nurturing role of an elementary teacher. On the other hand, 80 percent of principals are men, so children rarely see women as effective and competent administrators.

Discrimination within the schools is not limited to sex. B. R. McCandless (1969) finds

> discrimination rampant on subtle as well as obvious grounds. Pressing socialization needs, such as in the sexual-social area, are all but ignored. Lower class youngsters, minority group youngsters, nonconforming youngsters, borderline-ability youngsters—all are shamefully ignored or even openly discriminated against. The socialization record becomes worse as the child moves from first to twelfth grade (p. 811).

In considering early socialization, one must remember that the vast majority of research on sex-role development and socialization involves white middle-class populations. Whether these conclusions are generalizable to other subgroups is open to question. Many scholars and artists have written perceptive works on the socialization experiences of blacks (Wright, 1937; Baldwin, 1963; Brown, 1966; Billingsley, 1968; Ladner, 1971; Lerner, 1973), the lower class (Komarovsky, 1964; Seifer, 1973), Spanish-speaking minorities, Asian Americans, and American Indians. Major research data, however, are missing.

Role of Significant Others in Post-High School Plans

Socialization does not end once an individual reaches adolescence but continues through the secondary and postsecondary years and beyond. Male and female students go through several periods of socialization. As they pursue their education, they are socialized as scholars; when they enter careers or jobs, they are socialized as members of the profession or field. At each stage they learn the rules and the expected forms of behavior. The parents, teachers, counselors, and peers who affected them in early years continue to do so. These significant individuals play a part in the future plans and orientation of students of both sexes.

The Teacher

It is possible to evaluate the role of significant others by looking at both their attitudes and their impact as perceived by students. Rosenthal and Jacobson (1968), in their analysis of the impact of teacher attitudes on student behavior, indicated that teachers' favorable or unfavorable expectations can result in a corresponding increase or decrease in a pupil's intellectual performance. K. C. Christensen and W. E. Sedlacek's (1972) study of faculty attitudes toward university students showed that women and blacks are perceived more favorably than undergraduates in general. Blacks are perceived as serious, hard-working, outspoken students who should be kept in line more, while women are seen as the best, hardest-working, most creative students. While these findings are indeed positive, they indicate a stereotypic view of both groups.

Other studies show more negative but equally stereotypic findings. L. G. Garman and W. T. Platt (1974), in research with instructors from the elementary, secondary, and college levels, asked whether teachers, like mental health professionals (Broverman et al., 1970), describe healthy women differently from healthy adults whose sex is unspecified, but do not make this distinction between adults and healthy men. They also asked whether the sex of the teacher is related to the use of sex-role stereotypes. Their results indicated that at all levels educators' concepts of mature personality differ for men and women, and that these differences parallel sex-role stereotypes. Both male and female educators describe women less like mature adults than they do men, yet female educators see women as much closer to the adult standard than do male educators.

Holding stereotypes about students, one might argue, does not necessarily result in negative consequences. Pettigrew (1964) noted, however, that positive is as deleterious as negative stereotyping: It forces individuals into certain roles. S. Sue and H. L. Kitano (1973) listed several negative results of positive stereotypes: Asian-Americans are viewed as quiet, unobtrusive, hard-working, and intelligent—all positive characteristics. Yet this stereotype often results in Asian students' remaining passive, unquestioning, and obedient to conform to their teachers' expectations. When these students are rebellious or low achieving, they may have to contend with anger from teachers because they have violated the teachers' expectations. H. F. Pettigrew (1964) suggested that a self-fulfilling prophecy may operate with stereotypes that are rigidly and widely held. The self-fulfilling prophecy tends to make individuals behave in accordance with other persons' expectations; individuality within the group is limited.

Rosenthal and Jacobson, as well as K. G. Dickerson (1974), showed that stereotyping does affect student behavior. Dickerson asked female undergraduate and graduate students at four colleges to complete a questionnaire on their academic-vocational aspirations and on faculty and administrative perceptions of their academic-vocational roles. The results indicated that students with higher aspirations are more apt to be those who feel that faculty and administration have high expectations for them. Voluntary comments from these students indicated that they are influenced by the expectations that they perceive faculty and administration have for them, thus supporting the Pygmalion notion that a person's behavior is influenced by another's expectations (Dickerson, 1974).

The Counselor

Counselors' attitudes toward men and women are discussed in Chapter 5. In brief, their attitudes tend to follow stereotypic lines; that is, characteristics of the sexes are viewed as following prescribed patterns, and career options are often seen as limited to typically feminine or masculine occupations. Students' perceptions of their interactions with counselors are presented below, with similar data for interaction with other significant individuals in the secondary student's experience.

The Parent

In addition to treating the sexes differently, parents affect their adolescents' career development in indirect ways. Baruch (1972), investigating the reason why some women devalue feminine professional competence, indicated that the tendency to devalue is associated with having a nonworking mother.

Women whose mothers worked evaluate women's competence higher, regardless of any negative experience their mother may have had as a result of work. E. Almquist and S. S. Angrist (1971), investigating the effect of role models and reference groups on college women's career aspirations, found that career-oriented women have working mothers, have been exposed to occupational choices of male peers, and feel influenced by faculty members and occupational role models in choosing a career. Noncareer-oriented women have mothers who are more often active in leisure pursuits.

Student Perception of Interactions

While teachers and parents come into frequent contact with students, the counselors' contacts are less frequent. They all, however, have some impact on the students' post-high school plans. Their attitudes and values are likely to affect their interaction with students. Since no existing studies were found to address this issue, three data sources were examined for some understanding of how significant others affect students.

Project TALENT

The Project TALENT survey (see details in Appendix) indicated that boys have often discussed post-high school plans with their fathers, while girls have consulted with mothers, siblings, friends, and other adults. Counselors, teachers, principals, and clergy advise both sexes equally. What cannot be ascertained is whether these individuals seek high school students to give them advice or whether they are sought by the students. Fathers more often are sought by boys than by girls. This is an important observation when viewed in the light of Almquist and Angrist's (1971) findings that a masculine reference group is important in fostering career orientation in women.

When the class of 1960 was queried about the advice sought from teachers and counselors, men more often than women discussed college plans, high school work, and personal problems, while both discussed post-high school jobs with about equal frequency.

In a 1965 follow-up to the 1960 survey, participants were queried about important decisions that they regretted later. Of interest here is the relationship between students' contacts with their counselor and later satisfaction with decisions. For both sexes, "failure to obtain education after high school is inversely related to discussing higher education plans with the counselor" (Flanagan et al., 1964, pp. 6-8). More women who have infrequent discussions of college plans with counselors fail to *finish* college. More men than women are sorry that they have not attended college or that they dropped out. Women are more often sorry about their choice of college. There is, however, no systematic relationship between satisfaction with college decision and discussions with guidance counselors. J. C. Flanagan et al. noted that "this failure to find systematic trends where they would logically be expected poses some rather serious questions concerning the effectiveness of high school guidance programs" (pp. 8-13).

National Longitudinal Study

The National Longitudinal Study (NLS) provides insight into individuals with the most impact on high school students (see Appendix). Students in the study indicated which individuals had a strong influence on their choice of high school curriculum. Overall, parents have the greatest impact, while counselors and peers have some impact. Women seem more affected than men by parents, with minority students more affected than whites by all significant others.

In terms of students' post-high school plans, most important differences between subgroups occur by race rather than by sex, with black and Hispanic students relying more heavily than whites on parents, peers, other relatives, and counselors. Overall, women seem more affected than men by outside input, particularly from peers. White students are somewhat more likely to discuss their plans frequently with parents and peers than are minority students, suggesting that significant others are consulted in many cases but that their advice is not followed. Women appear to have more discussions of their plans with significant others and seem more affected by them.

Students were also asked specifically whether teachers or counselors try to influence their plans. A majority of both sexes is equally encouraged to go to college, and a majority does not perceive that counselors and teachers are trying to influence them toward vocational or technical schools. Men are more often encouraged to enter apprenticeships and the military, while women are more often encouraged to get jobs. The majority, however, perceives little intervention by teachers and counselors in terms of the above three options. On the whole, members of minority groups are encouraged more frequently than whites to seek every option. This finding may indicate that the counselor is aware that minority students are more receptive to input.

Exploratory Studies

Individual interviews were conducted during December 1974 with 70 students from seven high schools in metropolitan Los Angeles. Because one goal was to determine the major decision point in the postsecondary plans of students, tenth, eleventh, and twelfth graders were interviewed. Neither high school nor student selection was random, but subjects represent the complete range of socioeconomic levels and racial-ethnic backgrounds in the Los Angeles public school system. The student sample was 67 percent women and 33 percent men, 41 percent black, 14 percent Hispanic, 13 percent Asian-American, and 32 percent white. It included students whose parents' annual incomes range from $3,600 to $70,000.

Well over half the college-bound students identified a counselor as the most or second most helpful person in college-related matters. The second most frequently mentioned group is parents. The counselors are viewed as more helpful in inner-city schools, where many parents have not attended college and home situations often do not support college attendance. Students with older brothers or sisters who have attended college find them of help in making future plans. When asked who was most or second most helpful to them in selecting courses in high school, 65 percent of the boys and girls identified their counselor, and 30 percent mentioned "self." Once again, a pattern of greater dependence on the counselors emerges in the lower-SES schools, while the more affluent students are much more likely to depend on themselves or to be critical of counselors.

To determine who is viewed as the best resource person, students were asked whom they are most likely to see for information or advice about college and financial aid. Approximately eight out of ten students (88 percent of girls and 80 percent of boys) named their college advisor. Several of the more highly motivated students indicated that they contacted the financial aid office directly for more information, and one student in a high SES school had written to the Department of Health, Education, and Welfare for financial aid information. The college advisor is well regarded by almost all students. Typical comments are: "I don't know what I'd do without him" and "She is the most helpful—she knows everything."

These student attitudes are significantly different from many reported in the literature. Since the sample was not random, it was subject to bias. Counselors arranged the interviews and, in most cases, identified the students. Naturally, they would be more likely to select students with whom they were familiar, perhaps those with whom they had the greatest interaction. In some schools, however, the counselors did not select the students but arranged for classroom teachers to send students to the interviews. One counselor even recruited unfamiliar students from the hallway to participate in the study. The attitude toward counselors is not appreciably different in these situations, indicating that the bias of the sample cannot entirely account for the finding that counselors, especially college advisors, are good sources of information for most high school students.

As a group, the noncollege-bound and undecided students view counselors as the people most helpful in choosing high school classes and discussing college, and as the people to whom they would most likely turn for information about college and financial aid. Differences between girls and boys in the noncollege-bound group are not apparent, but the numbers (eight girls and four boys) are too small to warrant even preliminary conclusions. In fact, few conclusions can be drawn at this juncture about differential treatment by sex.

INTERNAL MECHANISMS

In addition to external socialization factors, the personal characteristics, motivation, and self-concept of students may affect guidance experiences. From previous experiences and their own aspirations and self-images, students develop perceptions and attitudes about the environment and their current and future roles. Evidence links sex-role perceptions, self-concept, and achievement motivation to achievement and life satisfaction (Connell and Johnson, 1970; Elman, Press, and Rosenkrantz, 1970; Hollender, 1972; Putnam and Hansen, 1972). An individual brings these internal variables to any guidance situation. Since these characteristics may determine whether an individual seeks counseling, which questions are raised, and how the information is interpreted and utilized, it is important for counselors and educational policy makers to understand the nature of these factors.

The interrelationship among these variables is complex. An individual's aspirations, self-concept, and opportunities help determine what activities he or she will attempt. Success or failure, in turn, affects self-esteem and future aspirations. These activities and the feeling about them build perceptions and attitudes that are incorporated into one's self-image and aspirations.

If the goal of counseling and guidance is to help students explore and understand themselves so that they may live more productive and satisfying lives, then achievement motivation and aspirations, self-concept and self-esteem, and student perceptions and attitudes are essential areas to explore. Not only must the counselor be well acquainted with the theoretical constructs of these characteristics, but he/she must also be sensitive to individual differences. The counselor can then be a major resource person, aiding the student in self-exploration and development. The counselor can also help students, teachers, and parents to understand others and to accept and encourage broader alternatives.

Achievement Motivation

Achievement motivation is the extent to which one is concerned with attaining excellence. Historically, most research in this area involves men. In recent years, however, researchers have examined two crucial questions that probe differential responses of men and women to achievement motivation: (1) Are women motivated to achieve to the same extent as men? and (2) Are women motivated in the same areas and for the same reasons as men? Similarities and differences in the nature and level of achievement motivation affect student choices and alternatives. Efforts to answer these questions have, however, resulted in contradictory findings, both in underlying theories and in the empirical evidence.

Theory

Work by D. C. McClelland et al. (1953) forms the theoretical basis for much research on achievement motivation. The authors conceptualize achievement motivation as a relatively stable personality disposition, learned in early childhood, to strive for success in any situation where standards of excellence are applicable and to feel pride about success and shame about failure. They perceive the motive to achieve as generalizing across achievement areas. According to their theory, this motive remains latent until it is aroused by situational cues; it is then activated when the individual believes that the consequences of his/her actions will lead to favorable or unfavorable evaluation. Once aroused, the motive resulted in achievement-oriented activity only if it is greater than the tendency to avoid failure.

According to a second model proposed by V. Crandall et al. (1964), there are three determinants of motivation in a given situation: expectancy of success, attainment value (the value attached to a particular type of achievement), and standards of performance. The minimum standard of performance is the lowest level an individual considers satisfactory.

Socialization

The level and direction of achievement motivation appear to be affected by sex-role definitions, orientations, and expectations. Sex-role orientation may cause individuals to be motivated to achieve only in areas that are appropriate to their sex. For example, women may be motivated to achieve in areas appropriate to their female sex-role definition rather than in "inappropriate" masculine domains.

Achievement needs may conflict with and be suppressed by affiliative needs (the need to seek the company of others). Some writers theorize that achievement behavior in women results from affiliative rather than achievement motivation. A. H. Stein and M. M. Bailey (1973) concluded, however, that this theory misinterprets the fact that social skill and interpersonal relations are often important areas of achievement for women. Although women may be more concerned than men with social approval and with achieving in social areas, this concern does not determine their achievement behavior.

"Feminine" personality attributes, such as nonassertiveness and dependency, may conflict with achievement motivation as it is usually manifested in intellectual and occupational contexts (Hoffman, 1972; Bem and Bem, 1973). Fear of success, a motive postulated by M. S. Horner (1972), may also conflict with the motive to achieve. Considered a stable personality trait, fear of success probably develops in early childhood and adolescence when a girl learns or expects that negative consequences will follow her success because of the masculine sex-typed nature of achievement and the personality qualities and behavior necessary for it.

Women have evolved numerous methods to reduce the conflict between achievement striving and the traditional female role. Some define achievement-related behavior as more feminine than others, and so they do not see their action as especially "out of role." Other women reduce the conflict by identifying with the masculine role. Satisfying achievement needs vicariously through the accomplishments of husbands and children is a common way of achieving while staying in role, as is pursuing a feminine career or remaining in a low-status occupational position. Concealing accomplishments (for example, reporting a lower grade than actually received), and reducing effort, particularly in a competitive situation, lessen the conflict for some women. Finally, a woman can "compensate" for her achievement striving by being feminine in appearance and behavior or by fulfilling all the functions of the traditional feminine role—wife/ mother/homemaker—as well as those of her career (Horner, 1972).

Why do so many girls and women experience this conflict between achievement striving and the feminine role, perceiving achievement as unfeminine? Stein and Bailey (1973), examining the literature on socialization to see how children learn the various achievement and behavior patterns, concluded that child-rearing practices conducive to feminine sex typing are frequently antagonistic to those that lead to achievement-oriented behavior. The aspects of child rearing that appear to facilitate achievement-oriented behavior in women are a moderate, but not high, level of warmth or nurturance, permissiveness, independence (especially emotional independence) and parental encouragement to achieve (including positive reinforcement, attempts at acceleration, criticism for lack of effort, and an achieving maternal model). Even if a girl's parents provide these conditions, significant others—peers, teachers, relatives—also affect her development with their expectations and reactions (Rosenthal and Jacobson, 1958; Levy, 1973). Adolescence, with its vulnerability to social pressure, is a crucial time for achievement motivation in females (Campbell and McKain, 1974). Not only do social pressures affect males and females differently, but among women there is also a differentiation effect across class, race, and ethnic lines (Hishiki, 1969; Johnson, 1970; Seifer, 1973; Astin, 1975).

Differential Aspirations

The level of aspiration of an individual may also serve to limit the occupational choices. Data from the National Longitudinal Study (NLS) facilitate identification of differences in educational preparation and aspirations on the basis of sex, race, and father's education (Fetters, 1975).

In the NLS study, in which students indicated the highest level of education they planned to attain, 20 percent of girls and 13 percent of boys indicated no plans past high school graduation.

Among low-SES students, blacks, independent of sex, are more likely than whites to pursue education at four-year institutions than in vocational schools. More black men (58 percent) and women (54 percent) whose fathers are not high school graduates plan to pursue college education than white men (49 percent) and women (49 percent) whose fathers are not graduates. They are less likely to pursue vocational training. If the father is a college graduate, the gap between types of postsecondary training widens. Higher proportions of the high-SES white than black students, however, plan collegiate education.

National surveys of black high school seniors conducted in 1971 and 1974 (NSSFNS, 1972) provided data on sex differences in degree aspirations. Of the high school students desiring a bachelor's degree or less in 1974, black women are more likely (16 percent) to seek technical certificates or associate degrees than black men (12 percent), but less likely to seek a bachelor's degree. Black women are more likely (28 percent) to seek master's degrees than black men (26 percent) but less likely (22 percent) to seek doctoral or professional degrees (24 percent). There appears to be a general increase in the level of aspiration from 1971 to 1974, especially for black women moving from master's to doctoral and professional degree aspirations.

An ongoing longitudinal survey of American higher educational institutions, the Cooperative Institutional Research Program (CIRP), yields information on degree and occupational aspirations of college freshmen. A comparison of male and female degree aspirations indicates that while women still have lower aspirations than men, the level, especially for professional degrees, is increasing. A similar comparison of black college students for 1968 and 1971 (Bayer, 1972; Bayer and Boruch, 1969) is consistent with degree aspirations of black high school students in the National Scholarship Service and Fund for Negro Students (NSSFNS) sample. While black men and women tended to have the same interest in a bachelor's degree in 1971, more women (38 percent) than men (32 percent) desired a master's and more men (26 percent) than women (19 percent) aspired to a doctoral or professional degree. Between 1968 and 1971 there was a slight shift in aspirations toward professional degrees. Based on NSSFNS data, this trend probably continued in 1974, perhaps becoming even more pronounced for black women than for black men.

A comparison of degree aspirations of all women who are entering college and of women 31 years of age and above reveals that, while older women make up less than 4 percent of the sample, their markedly lower degree aspirations indicate that they approach higher education with a different frame of reference than younger women. This subgroup may require different counseling programs and techniques.

The CIRP also indicates trends in career aspirations of college freshmen. Because of decreasing opportunities, there is a substantial decrease in the percentage of students, especially women, aspiring to careers in education. Women's aspirations are shifting to business and health. Men, who are shifting away from education careers, are also moving away from engineering. The fields to which men increasingly aspire are not clear from these data but some increased interest appears in the allied health area and in farming/forestry. Both men and women freshmen are increasingly undecided about careers (7 percent and 9 percent increases from 1973 to 1974). Certainly this reflects the ambiguous job market and highlights students' needs for guidance in understanding occupational opportunities and their educational requirements.

A similar, though less dramatic, trend appears for black high school and college students. Among black high school students, interest in education is decreasing and interest in artistic, health, and science areas is increasing. Black high school women in 1974 showed a dramatic surge of interest in business. For black college students, a drop in education career aspirations parallels increases in professional (doctor, lawyer) aspirations.

Women, regardless of race, still do not aspire to prestigious occupations as frequently as men, and stereotypic occupational preferences persist. The percentage of women aspiring to be engineers, lawyers, business executives, and doctors is from one-tenth to one-half that of men, whereas the reverse is true for elementary and secondary education and health and nursing occupations. Older women aspire to even less prestigious occupations than freshmen women: nursing, business, secretarial-clerical occupations, computer programming, and the like.

Attribution Theory

Differences in the nature and level of aspirations between men and women and among racial and ethnic groups appear in some studies. While such differences are attributed to varying achievement motivation, this relationship may be more assumption than fact. Frieze et al. (1975), reviewing research on achievement-oriented behavior, found that some studies attribute women's failure to achieve to internal factors. These authors think that external barriers are as important as internal psychological barriers, if not more important.

People with high expectations of success tend to perform better on achievement tasks. Because of widely held sex-role stereotypes, it is quite likely that women have lower generalized expectations of success than men. The course to which an individual attributes his/her success or failure influences future expectancies and subsequent achievement strivings.

Four causes of achievement outcome are ability, effort, luck, and task difficulty. Ability and effort are internal, while luck and task difficulty are external or environmental. Theoretically, maximum self-esteem would be associated with a tendency to make internal attributions for success and external or unstable attributions for failure. Women's attributions are generally external, often encouraged by modesty, low self-esteem, external locus of control, and fear of success. Individual differences, such as need for achievement, mediate attribution patterns, as do such situational factors as whether the task is competitive.

The expectations and attributions of others concerning women in achievement situations are also quite important: They can affect hiring, promotion, and other opportunities. Women's internal cognitive barriers to achievement, such as lower expectation of success, stem from cultural standards for behavior appropriate to the sexes.

Self-Concept

The image an individual develops of him/herself affects behavior and attitudes. In turn, new experiences affect self-concept. The manner in which information is processed and internalized to some extent depends on how consistent that information is with this self-image. To some degree alternatives are considered, decisions made, and level of success expected in light of what the individual knows about him/herself.

The nature and level of the student's self-concept are, then, important to effective guidance and counseling. Counselors, to provide pertinent educational and career guidance, need to understand the interrelationships of self-concept, aspirations, and achievement. Furthermore, counselors must be aware of possible differences in the nature of self-concepts for certain subgroups and the implications these differences have for guidance experiences.

Recent studies focus on self-concept as a mediating variable in achievement in efforts to understand the reasons for women's lower aspirations and achievement. From these studies, which demonstrate the lower evaluation of feminine traits and products (Broverman et al., 1970; Rosenkrantz et al., 1968; Goldberg, 1968), one would expect women to hold low or negative views of their worth.

Some studies have reported that women set lower aspirations and goals for themselves (Watley, 1971) and that views and expectations of others influence young women's orientation to academic endeavors (Crandall et al., 1964; Brindley, 1971; Entwisle and Greenberger, 1972). Others have suggested that women have lower self-esteem than men. Berger (1968) concluded that the self-evaluation of women is partially contingent on their degree of certainty that other people like them. This implies that women's self-esteem is shaped by the messages they receive from significant others, rather than by tests of their own competencies. Although self-esteem might increase from successful testing, if the competencies are perceived as incongruent with "feminine" behavior or approval, the impact on self-evaluation might be negative.

Maccoby and Jacklin (1974), who examined 30 studies on self-esteem, did not find any sex differences on this trait. They concluded that "there is no overall difference between the sexes in self-esteem, but there is a male cluster among college students made up of greater self-confidence when undertaking new tasks, and a greater sense of potency, specifically including the feeling that one is in a position to determine the outcomes of sequences of events that one participates in" (p. 158).

The effect these self-perceptions have on motivation, achievement, persistence, and career development and commitment, however, remains undetermined. The impact of different college environments and experiences on the growth of self-esteem must also be determined, since a positive overall self-image, as well as accurate accounts of one's intellectual competencies and leadership qualities, are determinants of success in the world of work.

Students in the NLS answered two questions that reflect self-image and expectations. One indicated agreement with statements reflecting views about themselves in relationship to aspects of life. Even though more men take a positive attitude toward themselves (88 percent men; 84 percent women), more women are satisfied with themselves (77 percent women; 74 percent men). Moreover, more men (94 percent) than women (90 percent) say, "I am able to do things as well as most other people." Despite these small differences, overall, young persons see themselves in positive terms. An examination of differences in life goals of high school men and women indicated that more men consider success in work an important objective, whereas a higher percentage of women viewed the right mate and family life as important. Lots of money and a leadership role are more important for men.

The CIRP's 1974 freshmen survey indicated that men and women differ in self-ratings, with men rating themselves higher on academic achievement-oriented traits and women rating themselves higher on "artistic ability," "cheerfulness," "understanding of others," "writing ability," and "sensitivity to criticism," none of which is particularly achievement directed (Astin et al., 1974).

An examination of the self-ratings of black students entering colleges revealed lower self-ratings for black compared with white men and women on "academic ability," "mathematical ability," "mechanical ability," and, to some extent, "originality." Ratings on "drive to achieve" and "intellectual self-confidence" are comparable, while ratings on "popularity in general" and "popularity with the opposite sex" are higher for black than for white students.

Compared with white women, black women rate themselves lower on "artistic ability" and "math ability" and higher on "drive to achieve," "popularity in general," "popularity with the opposite sex," "intellectual self-confidence," and "social self-confidence." Compared with black men, black women rate themselves higher on "drive to achieve" but lower on "leadership," "math ability," "mechanical ability," "popularity with the opposite sex," and "intellectual and social self-confidence."

In a comparison of women over 31 in two-year institutions with all college women in all institutions, older women rate themselves lower than all other women on a number of the academic and achievement variables. In part, this is because being away from school-related tasks tends to undermine their self-confidence. Also, this sample represents adult women attending two-year institutions. Academic and achievement ratings tend to be lower for students at two- than at four-year institutions, independent of sex. The older women rate themselves lower than all freshmen women on "academic ability," "math ability," "originality," and "writing ability." These women also tend to rate themselves lower than men on academic and achievement traits.

Closely allied to self-ratings are life goals, since they reflect needs and motivations for educational attainment and occupational development. When asked about the "person they would most like to be," black women aspire to be educators and creative or performing artists, while black men select roles as businessmen, athletes, and scientists.

Women as a whole give higher priority to "influence social values," "raise a family," "help others in difficulty," "original writing and artistic works," "develop a philosophy of life," and "participate in community action." Men list "obtain recognition from colleagues," "be an authority in my field," "be very well off financially," and "be successful in my own business."

Student Attitudes

Students' conceptions of sex roles and the world of work are not simply the results of high school and post-high school experiences; they evolve from earliest childhood. As the individual moves through high school and beyond, these attitudes continue to evolve. Attitudes affect the alternatives that the individual perceives as available and, ultimately, his/her choices. When a student seeks information about career options, completes an interest inventory, or discusses perceptions and aspirations with a counselor, sex-role attitudes will affect the outcome of the guidance activity.

Differential Sex-Role Perceptions

Children as young as 30 to 40 months are aware of the sex linkage of many common items (clothing, tools, and so forth) and prefer same-sex articles (Vener and Snyder, 1966). Second-, sixth-, and twelfth-grade students, in a study by A. H. Stein and J. Smithell (1969), saw certain skills as feminine and others as masculine. These standards became more definite from second to twelfth grade. The sex-age interaction suggested that changes in sex-role standards result primarily from learning what is and is not appropriate for one's own sex. In addition to changing over time, attitudes vary among students in one age group, according to a study of ninth-grade students' attitudes toward women's work roles by D. R. Entwisle and E. Greenberger (1972). Boys and girls differ in their conceptions of women's role. Both sexes disapprove of women's holding men's jobs, but boys consistently hold more traditional opinions. While black students are less opposed than white students to women's working, they are just as negative toward women's doing the same work as men. While daughters of blue-collar workers are more traditional than inner-city girls in their views of women's roles, high-IQ sons and daughters of blue-collar workers are the most nontraditional. The greatest difference between boys' and girls' views appears among middle-class white students, with high-IQ middle-class boys the most traditional.

B. F. Turner and C. Turner (1974) identified a similar pattern of differential sex-role attitudes among college students. No significant difference appears in the evaluations of "most women" by black men and women and white women. White men, however, evaluate women in significantly more negative terms than do white women on instrumentality (masculine) factors, but not differently on emotionality (feminine) factors. F. Rosenkrantz et al. (1968) examined the relationship between sex-role stereotypes and self-concepts among college students. Men and women appear to agree strongly about differences between the sexes and more frequent high evaluation of stereotypic masculine characteristics by both sexes. Women feel negative about their own worth, compared with that of men.

The emerging picture is one of pervasive stereotypic sex-role attitudes among high school and college students. Such attitudes circumscribe the options available to both sexes. Students' awareness of traditionally appropriate sex roles, not only in terms of work but also in terms of personal characteristics, self-concepts, and self-esteem, indicates that high intergenerational stability of sex-role definitions exists (Vener and Snyder, 1966). This stability may work against egalitarianism between the sexes.

Still, the literature offers some encouragement. D. S. Dorn (1970) found that a majority of men and women think that the double standard has declined and women have more egalitarian relationships with men. While both men and women agree that the ideal female role would include an egalitarian relationship with men, a companion-complement marriage with mutual decisions, and a life style that allows a woman to develop to her full capacity, men have difficulty acknowledging this ideal in their own behavior. In a study of attitudes toward sex-role division in adult occupations across four age groups, Shepard and Hess (1975) found that, in every group except kindergarteners, females are significantly more "liberal" than males. In terms of age differences, both kindergarten and adult subjects are relatively traditional. The attitudes of today's adults have probably influenced their child-rearing practices and, subsequently, their children's attitudes. Considerable nontraditionalism exists among eighth-grade and college students, an intergenerational break in sex-role attitudes that suggests positive implications for future child-rearing practices and for more egalitarian conceptions of adult sex-roles.

Women's Perceptions of Men's Beliefs

As one's own sex-role perceptions affect one's attitudes, so also can one's beliefs about significant others' perceptions affect attitudes and behavior. Hawley (1971) hypothesized that women are influenced in their career choice by what they believe men think is appropriate. Women's perceptions of men's views vary with career group and marital status. A series of studies (Steinmann, 1959, 1963; Steinmann and Fox, 1966) that examined sex differences in perceptions of the "average woman" and the "ideal woman" showed that women believe that the ideal woman should strive for a balance between self-realization and intrafamily nurturing. But women's view of men's ideal woman is significantly more family oriented and personally subordinated. The authors noted that some women do not seek work roles because they believe that men prefer traditional homemakers, when in fact men prefer as their ideal a balanced woman. They are especially positive about women being active outside the home to fulfill themselves. On specific statements about marriage and children, however, men are less certain and often contradict their general opinions. In a similar study of college students' perceptions of "average man" and "average woman" (Kaplan and Goldman, 1973), both men and women indicated that the average man views women in a more traditional manner than does the average woman. But women perceive a greater difference between female stereotypes held by men and women than men do. Men appear somewhat more conservative about women's role, but their attitudes may not be as conservative or restrictive as women believe. Some possible causes for women's misconception of men's perceptions are women's lower valuation of women's traits and the contradictory cues that women receive from men.

The potential impact on women's behavior of such perceptions or misperceptions by women of men's attitudes is the concern of Farmer and Bohn (1970). Women in their study completed the Strong Vocational Interest Blank (SVIB) under standard directions. Then they took it again, pretending that men have "come of age": that they like intelligent women, that men and women are promoted equally, and that raising a family is possible for a career woman. Career scales increased and homemaker scales decreased significantly under conflict-reducing directions. Attitudinal response does influence SVIB scores and, consequently, it may influence options and choices.

Some variation, however, appears among women's perceptions of male attitudes. Women preparing for careers in male-dominated areas (math, science) and counselors-in-training believe that men make little differentiation in male-female work roles, behavior, or attitudes. But students preparing to teach believe that men divide work, behavior, and attitudes into male and female categories (Hawley, 1972). Similarly, S. R. Vogel et al. (1970) found that both men and women with employed mothers see fewer differences between masculine and feminine roles than those with homemaker mothers. Women's more than men's perceptions tend to be strongly influenced by maternal employment. Maternal employment also tends to raise estimations of one's own sex about characteristics considered socially desirable for the opposite sex. Sex-role perceptions are affected by parental role behavior and by one's own occupational aspirations.

Attitudes toward Professional Competence

Women's attitudes toward their professional competence are consistent and disturbing. P. Goldberg (1968) asked college women to evaluate six articles, two written by authors in traditionally male occupations, two by authors in traditionally female occupations, and two in neutral occupations. Half the women were told that the authors were men; the other half were told that the authors were women. Regardless of professional area, works attributed to male authors were evaluated more highly by this group.

G. K. Baruch (1972), in a similar study of college women, found that the tendency to devalue feminine competence is associated with having a non-working mother. Approval of a dual-life role (family and career) depends on the mother's endorsement of the dual-role pattern and on how successfully a working mother has integrated the roles. N. T. Feather and J. G. Simon (1975) found a similar pattern among high-SES high school girls. In reacting to male and female success in various occupations, these girls overestimate the achievement of successful compared with unsuccessful males and depreciate achievements of successful compared with unsuccessful females. They view an easy course of study as the cause of female success, but attribute male success to ability. They see successful men as likely to continue to succeed, to be praised, and to be famous, and as unlikely to wonder if they are normal or to worry about studying too much. They believe that the reverse is true about successful women.

These studies imply that success and achievement are masculine attributes. When a woman is successful, either her achievement is devalued or a multitude of negative consequences is associated with her success. Since success by women is not highly valued even by other women, high self-motivation and an internalized reward system are required for women to seek success. Such attitudes toward success in competitive situations not only mitigate against women's desires to seek and to achieve success, but also establish a potential failure and demasculinizing situation for men. Success defeminizes women; failure demasculinizes men. Such attitudes are highly dysfunctional for any individual regardless of sex.

Vocational Preferences

Just as students' career goals or preferences are products of past experiences, these characteristics are likely to grow and change as students acquire new experiences. While the data on career preferences of different age groups are still sketchy, some trends important to counselors are emerging. In a study of fifth graders (Iglitzen, 1973), girls stated varied career aspirations, although these aspirations are heavily weighted toward traditional female occupations. In describing a typical day in their future, however, these girls emphasized marriage and family activities, whereas boys focused on job or career. Girls show a limited awareness of what a career or dual-role orientation involves. In a study of kindergarten and sixth-grade students, both boys and girls preferred careers within the usual stereotypes (Schlossberg and Goodman, 1972a). R. Mowsesian (1972) documented shifts in educational and career aspirations among high school women from ninth and tenth to eleventh and twelfth grades. Among these women, emphasis on four-year-college education decreases, while emphasis on two-year-college education increases. Occupational preferences shift from professional and semiprofessional areas to more evenly distributed preferences across all occupational categories. The proportion of women planning to marry doubles.

L. W. Harmon (1971) found that the most persistent career preferences for college women (after housewife) are the typically feminine education and social service. The least persistent preferences involve occupations that require unusual talents, long periods of training, or short noncollege training. A small sample of college women contacted by A. Steinmann (1970) generally do not think work is very important. The majority plans either not to work or to work only if it is financially necessary. Differences in career preferences and expectations exist between black and white college women (Turner and McCaffery, 1974). Black women expect more occupational involvement than they prefer, while white women prefer more occupational involvement than they expect. Variables expressing external control predict level of career expectations for blacks, whereas variables expressing internal control predict high career expectations among whites. Differences between the groups may stem from socialization histories, necessitating the study of career antecedents separately by race. While none of these samples is representative, the studies suggested major hypotheses about women's career development and preferences that warrant further investigation. For example, at what age do individuals begin to solidify career plans? What types of information are involved, and how can new information be supplied to the individual to broaden the alternatives? What variations in women's career development and preferences exist among geographic regions, SES groups, and racial groups? What unique socialization factors and environmental structures contribute to these variations? The results will carry major implications for counseling and guidance services for women.

SUMMARY AND IMPLICATIONS FOR
GUIDANCE AND COUNSELING

Both external factors (the school system, the media, and parental behavior) and internal mechanisms (self-concept, achievement motivation, and sex-role stereotypes) contribute to socialization and counteract change.

It is well known that certain behaviors are sex typed, due largely to children's learning early the behavior and characteristics deemed appropriate for males or females. Other sex differences are myths and still others require additional evidence before their reliability can be ascertained. Among the external factors that affect young children are parents who encourage their children to develop sex-typed interests or who provide them with sex-typed toys. They discourage their children, especially their sons, from inappropriate sex-typed behaviors and activities (Maccoby and Jacklin, 1974).

Children's literature and television are also major sources of information for preschool children. Analyses of children's books and of elementary, secondary, and college textbooks have revealed that women are grossly underrepresented. Where women appear, traditional sex-role stereotypes are reinforced (Weitzman et al., 1972; Women on Words and Images, 1972). Prime-time television communicates the message "that there are more men around, that they are dominant, authoritative, and competent" (p. 30). Women hold traditional jobs, are dependent, and have more negative characteristics. These stereotypes are even more explicit in commercials (Women on Words and Images, 1975).

The educational system as a whole deals unequally with the two sexes, according to some (Harrison, 1973; Frazier and Sadker, 1973; Women on Words and Images, 1972; MacLeod and Silverman, 1973). In a sense, the educational system mirrors society: In a society that deals unequally with men and women, it is not surprising that the schools deal unequally with boys and girls. The teacher may allow different forms of behavior by the two sexes and may treat boys and girls differently. Boys receive more attention, both positive and negative, more praise, more instruction, and often more encouragement to be creative. Girls are trained to be docile and conforming. As early as kindergarten, curricula and activities may not be the same for each sex: For example, both sexes may not have equal access to all play materials in the classroom (Sears and Feldman, 1966; Levy, 1973).

An analysis of data from the NLS (Fetters, 1975) indicated that in the high school years, students may be strongly affected by those around them. Boys often discuss post-high school plans with their fathers, while girls consult with mothers, siblings, friends, and other adults. Counselors, teachers, principals, and clergy give advice to both sexes equally. Overall, females appear to have more discussions about their plans with significant others and seem more affected by the advice than males. In fact, both sexes are equally encouraged to go to college and neither group perceives that counselors and teachers are trying to influence it toward vocational or technical schools.

A review of internal mechanisms that interfere with changes in sex-role behavior indicated that sex-role perceptions, self-concept, and achievement motivation all have important restraining effects on men and women. For instance, the level and direction of achievement motivation appear to be affected by sex-role definitions, orientations, and expectations, and thus sex-role orientation may cause individuals to be motivated to achieve only in areas that are appropriate to their sex (Horner, 1972).

High school girls appear to have lower educational aspirations than boys. The NLS indicated that more girls (20 percent) than boys (13 percent) have no plans for education past high school. Other studies (Watley, 1971) also indicated that women set lower aspirations for themselves and that the views and expectations of others influence young women's orientation toward academic endeavors (Crandall et al., 1964; Brindley, 1971; Entwisle and Greenberger, 1972). Self-esteem also contributes to the lower aspirations of women. Results of the CIRP 1974 freshman survey indicated that men and women differ in self-esteem, with men rating themselves high on traits oriented to academic achievement and women rating themselves higher on "artistic ability," "cheerfulness," "understanding of others," "writing ability," and "sensitivity to criticism," none of which is particularly achievement directed (Astin et al., 1974).

The CIRP survey indicated that men's life goals are determined more by extrinsic needs and interests, whereas women's objectives are more intrinsic in nature. More high school and college men consider success in their work an important objective, whereas a higher percentage of high school and college women thinks finding the right mate and having a family life are important life objectives. High school students of both sexes also differ in their conceptions of women's roles (Turner and Turner, 1974): Both groups disapprove of women's holding men's jobs, but boys consistently hold more conservative opinions. While acceptance of women working seems to be increasing, women's career options are restricted largely to traditional feminine areas. Women believe that the ideal woman should strive for a balance between self-realization and intra-family nurturing. In contrast, women's view of men's ideal woman is significantly more family oriented and personally subordinated. This belief inhibits some women in seeking working roles because they believe that men prefer traditional homemakers. Finally, success and achievement are considered masculine attributes (Feather and Simon, 1975). When a woman is presented as successful, either her achievement is devalued or a multitude of negative consequences is associated with her success. Since success by women is not highly valued even by other women, it requires high self-motivation and an internalized reward system for women to seek success.

Facilitating students' life adjustment, role clarification, and self-understanding is the purpose of guidance and counseling. Evaluation of sex fairness or sex bias in guidance and counseling at the secondary level and beyond is complicated by the socialization process. Students at these levels, as well as counselors, teachers, parents, and others, have learned behaviors, attitudes, and aspirations appropriate to their sex, internalizing cultural sex stereotypes. The institutions within which they function are products of these cultural conditions. Analysis of overt sex discrimination in counselor attitudes and counseling materials is not sufficient to determine the dimension of sex bias confronting both boys and girls in high school and later. Knowledge of the nature of the sex stereotypes that children have internalized through earlier socialization and of what other socializing agents—parents, teachers, books, movies, television, peers—are currently teaching students about their appropriate sex roles is essential to evaluate the success of counseling and guidance in optimizing an individual's alternatives regardless of sex.

While discriminatory hiring practices or college admissions policies can be outlawed, attitudes cannot be legislated. Stereotypes are exceedingly difficult to change.

> If a generalization (stereotype) about a group of people is believed, whenever a member of the group behaves in the expected way the observer notes it and his belief is confirmed and strengthened; when a member of the group behaves in a way that is not consistent with the observer's expectations, the instance is likely to pass unnoticed and the observer's generalized belief is protected from disconfirmation (Maccoby and Jacklin, 1974, p. 355).

Here the role of education and guidance becomes crucial. To overcome stereotypes that arbitrarily limit the options of either sex, a thoughtful, consistent, and thorough plan of education, not only for children but also for counselors, teachers, parents, employers and government agencies, is necessary. Until these groups are convinced that nursing is an appropriate career for boys as well as girls and that engineering is equally appropriate for both, there is little hope of changing the labor market structure. Until girls are encouraged to explore their potential for assertiveness and independence and boys their potential for empathy and compassion, the whole range of human feelings and behavior will not be equally available and acceptable for all.

Moreover, internal barriers to female achievement must be documented. The need for further research on differential achievement motivation between the sexes and among racial and ethnic groups is clear. Women and minorities, at this point, are not attaining academic degrees and occupational status—societal measures of achievement motivation—in proportion to their numbers. The causes must be pinpointed: Do women underachieve because they are achieving in other areas or because they have a low need to achieve? Do societal expectations inhibit their achievement strivings?

These issues have serious implications for guidance and counseling. If a woman is gratified through her current activities, her level of motivation may be satisfactory and, therefore, does not need to be the focus in guidance experiences. If internal or external barriers to women's achievement exist, however, these barriers and the methods to overcome them are important concerns for counselors. If these barriers are arbitrarily limiting women's self-understanding and opportunities for a satisfying life, the counselor is obligated to explore these barriers with women students. This same rationale applies to minority group students.

Self-concept and its interrelationship with achievement is the focus of much research. Researchers hypothesize that lower self-esteem and less expectation of success account for women's lower aspirations and achievement. On most measures of self-esteem, however, women show at least as much satisfaction with themselves as men do. Self-concept and life goals do have implications for the alternatives the individual considers and the choices he/she makes about educational preparation and careers. Counselors must avoid stereotypes related to the nature and impact of self-concept. Some commonly held beliefs are myths; others lend themselves to interpretations that arbitrarily limit individual options. Counselors must expose these myths and stereotypes, expand knowledge about the nature and impact of a self-concept, and help students develop self-concepts congruent with their full potential.

CHAPTER

3

WOMEN'S ACCESS TO AND PARTICIPATION IN EDUCATION

The role of counselors can be critical in the educational and career development of women. The expectation is that counselors understand such internal mechanisms as self-concept, achievement motivation, and sex-role socialization (Chapter 2), and recognize how external factors and institutional practices affect women. It is important that counselors understand the issues involved in discrimination in women's access to and participation in education.

Equal access to postsecondary education means an opportunity to attend the two- or four-year institution, proprietary school, or vocational institution that can prepare a person for an occupation or life style commensurate with his or her abilities, interests, and talents, and that can provide those experiences for personal and social growth necessary to achieve self-realization. Full participation in postsecondary education does not, of course, imply that every person should get a doctorate. It does mean that every person should make full use of his/her talents, not only those present at birth but also those acquired and developed in elementary and secondary school.

One way to define access operationally is to examine the actual participation rates of men and women in postsecondary programs. Though such statistics can give only a sketchy picture, they at least allow one to ascertain the extent to which women are taking advantage of all available educational opportunities.

A student's high school preparation—especially the program taken and the grades achieved—is clearly related to his/her educational plans and may even determine access to postsecondary institutions. The choice and achievement of a high school program are influenced by family and teachers, as well as peer pressures and expectations, SES, and counseling experiences. The choice of a college and a major affects later career choice and development. Thus, by looking at participation rates of men and women in different types of postsecondary education institutions and in different fields of study, one can infer the relative ease of access enjoyed by men and women.

HIGH SCHOOL PREPARATION AND EDUCATIONAL PLANS

National Longitudinal Study (NLS) data based on the high school class of 1972 revealed some notable differences between the sexes and among racial and ethnic groups in the type of high school program taken. For instance, the sexes are sharply segregated within vocational-technical programs: 21 percent of the women, compared with only 3 percent of the men, are taking business and office courses; and 11 percent of the men, compared with only 1 percent of the women, are concentrated in trade or industrial areas.

High school grades are usually considered crucial in the college admissions process and thus affect access to postsecondary education. Girls make considerably better high school grades than boys, yet fewer girls plan to attend graduate or professional school. The dynamics of this discrepancy are complex but, plainly, the lower aspirations of women are not explained by their grades.

The particular subjects studied in high school also affect access to postsecondary education. The student with little or no preparation in mathematics and science is not eligible for a technical program and is unlikely to be sought after by an engineering department. A smaller proportion of girls take five or more semesters of mathematics and science courses (although girls make slightly better grades in these courses than boys). This underrepresentation in mathematics and science, and its consequences, are attributed in part to social expectations of male superiority in math and sciences and in part to women's perceptions of the role of such courses in their future. Women often do not see how this preparation would permit them more educational and career options later. Girls are more likely than boys to take English and foreign language in high school—preparation that usually leads to an arts and humanities rather than a science major in college. Thus this channeling process narrows the options of women early in their lives, confining them to traditionally "female" fields.

A disturbing number of talented students are "lost" between high school and college. According to NLS data, sizable proportions of students who believe they have the ability to do college work are not planning to attend college. For instance, although three-fourths of the female respondents think that they are capable of completing college, fewer than half (45 percent) plan to attend. To prevent this talent loss between high school and college, more knowledge is needed about why students who think that they are capable of college work fail to go to college. What obstacles hinder them? Are the obstacles different for different groups of students?

The NLS data indicate that lack of money is an all-too-prominent reason. For instance, about one-fourth of the students who do not plan to continue their education expect to work full time. Although many said that their future plans require no further education, that they do not like school, or that they want a break from it, almost one in three men and women said that they need to earn money before they can pay for further education.

Poor grades or low scores on college admissions tests are another major reason for the failure to continue education. More men (24 percent) than women (15 percent) cited this reason. About half the women, but only one-third of the men, indicated that they could not afford a college or university education.

The reasons that students give for not continuing their education full time the year after high school graduation vary by sex. More women say they are not continuing by choice: Their plans simply do not call for more schooling. More men cite financial considerations. Apparently, for those who must support themselves and, in some cases, their families as well, even low- or no-tuition community colleges are prohibitively expensive because of forgone income. More men are prevented from continuing their education by poor high school grades or test scores. Men are also more likely to suffer from a lack of information about admissions requirements, college costs, and even the availability of a college.

The reasons for choosing a particular college vary somewhat by sex. Women are more interested in the academic program and reputation of the institution, including its admissions standards. They are also more concerned about costs and the availability of financial aid. This concern may reflect the parents' greater willingness to pay for a son's education than for a daughter's. Given the heavier dependence of women on their parents for financial support in college (it is pertinent here that women are more likely to look to their parents for advice in selecting a college) and their greater difficulty in earning money to pay for their education (Bengelsdorf, 1974), the parental attitude that higher priority should be given to educating a son puts women at a disadvantage. Despite their higher grades, they are less likely to go to college, and those who do attend may be more likely to select a less expensive, less prestigious institution than they would otherwise have chosen. These issues are explored in greater detail later.

COLLEGE ENROLLMENTS

According to the National Center for Educational Statistics (NCES), 1.53 million men and 1.58 million women graduated from high school in the academic year 1973-74. In fall 1974, 980,000 men and 870,000 women enrolled in higher education institutions as first-time, degree-credit students. If all these students came directly from high school, 64 percent of men and 56 percent of women high school graduates were continuing their education. Although women lagged behind men in college enrollments, the picture is not totally discouraging: College enrollment among women has increased dramatically over the past decade, just about doubling between 1964 and 1973 (U.S. Bureau of the Census, 1975a).

In fall 1974, 4.9 million men and 4 million women were working toward a college degree. It is well known that, as the educational level rises, the proportion of women enrolled decreases: Thus, women constituted 45 percent of two-year college enrollments, 43 percent of four-year college enrollments, and 42 percent of graduate enrollments (*Chronicle of Higher Education*, 1975).

Distribution of Students Among Institutions

A critical issue related to access is the type of institution that a student attends. Attending a prestigious and affluent institution has obvious advantages: Not only does the institution offer the student rich learning experiences, but it also may provide "fringe benefits," in that it facilitates a student's admission to graduate or professional school and to high-status occupations (Astin and Bayer, 1972). Do women, who generally make better grades than men and score about as well on aptitude tests, enter high-quality institutions in the same proportions as men? They constitute 45 percent of all college enrollments; what is their proportion in these elite institutions?

To answer these questions, an analysis was conducted using (1) data from an institutional selectivity index, developed by the research staff of the Cooperative Institutional Research Program (CIRP) and based on the aptitude test scores of students at a given institution, merged with (2) data collected during fiscal 1972 and 1973 by the Higher Education General Institutional Surveys (HEGIS), based on 2,492 higher education institutions. The merged file provided information on the following institutional characteristics: public versus private control; selectivity; affluence, measured by expenditures per student; and level of faculty salary.

The analysis showed that women are concentrated in smaller, less selective, and less affluent institutions, where median faculty salaries are relatively low. Were the distribution equitable, one would expect them to constitute 45 percent of the students at any institution, regardless of type. But they make up only 37 percent of the student body at highly selective public universities, and only 29 percent at highly selective private universities. Instead of being evenly distributed among institutional types, they are concentrated at Catholic institutions and at private, medium-sized, two-year colleges.

It seems reasonable that the more an institution spends per student for educational facilities and resources, the richer and more substantial the educational experience. Women lose out here, since they are less likely to attend affluent institutions. It also seems reasonable that faculty salaries are an index to faculty quality and thus to educational excellence. Here too women are slighted, since they attend institutions where median salaries are low. The concentration of women students in these institutions may reflect, in part, a higher concentration of women faculty at these institutions, since evidence indicates that women faculty, whatever their worth, are consistently paid lower salaries than their male counterparts (Astin and Bayer 1972; Bayer and Astin, 1975).

Although this analysis indicates that discrimination against women exists, its precise nature and causes are uncertain. Do elite institutions have policies and practices that exclude women? Are women discouraged from attending these institutions by their parents, teachers, counselors, friends? Do they lack confidence in their ability to succeed in a highly selected institution and thus do not apply? Or, conversely, do they fear the possible side effects of success at such institutions?

Another type of institution where women are drastically underrepresented is the institute of technology and engineering. Enrollment figures for 36 technical institutions reveal that at none do women constitute more than 35 percent of the students; the mean percentage of women at these institutions is 12.7 percent. Again, the analysis does not explain whether the causes of this underrepresentation lie with the institutions, society, or the women themselves. That the situation may be changing is evidenced by increased enrollments of women in the technical and professional programs actively recruiting them (Boyer, 1973).

College Major and Career Plans

Just as a student's selection of a program in high school limits his/her choice of a college major, so a student's choice of a college major limits his/her access to various occupations. The choice of a major, then, may be significant for one's future.

Women are most likely to select education or business as a probable college major. Generally, the popularity of such traditionally female fields as education, English, humanities, and fine arts has declined somewhat among women, whereas the nontraditional fields of business, biological sciences, agriculture, and "other" technical and nontechnical fields have grown in popularity. Black women have shown an interest in a business major for a longer period of time than women in general, and only about half as many black women plan to major in education. Though the growing tendency to choose nontraditional major fields may indicate that women are now willing to consider more options, the most popular fields among women are, except for business, traditional: education, nonmedical health fields, social science, and "other" nontechnical fields.

In contrast, the first four choices of men are business, engineering, "other" non-technical, and technical fields.

What are the characteristics of the women who choose nontraditional majors? Using data from the 1972 CIRP freshman survey to study the tiny proportion of women who plan to major in engineering, E. I. Holmstrom (1975) gave the following description:

> Basically, the women who wanted to major in engineering among 1972 freshmen were younger and brighter than other students; came from a mid-income family with well-educated parents; had high academic aspirations, and differed from other students, both men and women, in some of their attitudes and life goals (pp. 3-4).

In short, women who pioneer by majoring in traditionally male fields tend to be bright and assertive, with high aspirations.

Do probable college majors correspond to career plans? In 1974, the proportion of men planning to enter the three most popular careers among men—business, engineering, and medicine—corresponded closely to the proportion choosing the appropriate undergraduate majors. Among men, farming or forestry and the nonmedical health fields became somewhat more popular as career choices over the 1966-74 period, whereas careers in secondary education and engineering dropped in popularity. Women planned careers in nonmedical health fields, art, and teaching in the same proportions as they planned to major in the corresponding fields of study. Almost twice as many proposed to major in business as aspired to a career in this field, but even so, business, along with nursing, grew more popular over time as a career choice among women. Both elementary and secondary teaching became less popular, undoubtedly because of job scarcity. Despite some changes over time towards greater freedom from stereotypic choices, men were still primarily interested in traditionally "male" business and professional fields, and women were preparing themselves for traditionally "female" occupations. The increased interest of women in business (as reflected in the 16 percent who selected it as their probable college major) is somewhat vitiated in that only about half planned to use this training.

Degree Attainment

In 1973-74, women earned 45 percent of the bachelor's degrees, up one percentage point from 1971-72. Only in the traditionally female fields did they earn more than half the bachelor's degrees. But degree attainment does not necessarily guarantee employment: in the case of job-related majors, such as education and library science, these women faced a tight labor market. Other major fields in which women constituted a majority of those receiving bachelor's degrees, such as foreign languages and fine and applied arts, offered few employment possibilities. Only for women in the health fields and in home economics did job prospects seem favorable.

What of the future? First-time degree-credit enrollment, expressed as a percentage of the 18-year-old population, reached its highest point for both men and women in 1969 and 1970. Since then, the percentages have declined. It has been projected that the percentage of 18- and 19-year-olds attending college will level off at the 1973 figure and remain constant through 1983 (Simon and Frankel, 1975). Women are expected to constitute 46 percent of total degree-credit enrollment in all institutions of higher education and 44 percent in four-year institutions in 1983. The proportion of bachelor's degrees earned by women is expected to increase by 3 percentage points from 45 percent to 48 percent. Overall increases are expected in the number of social science and humanities degrees. Will women remain in the same fields as in the past, or will they diversify and enter nontraditional fields? If the latter is to occur, institutions bear much responsibility for making efforts to encourage women to enter fields that heretofore have always been male territory.

In 1973-74, women earned 9 percent of the first professional degrees (law, dentistry, medicine, theology, veterinary medicine, chiropody, optometry, and osteopathy), 44 percent of the master's degrees, and 19 percent of the doctorates. Women earned more than half the master's degrees in only six fields: in descending order, home economics, library science, foreign languages, education, health fields, and letters. Women also earned the majority of bachelor's degrees in these fields, but the proportion of the total earned by women decreased in every case from 1 percentage point in letters to 17 percentage points in the health professions.

At the doctoral level, women earned the majority of degrees in only one field, home economics. They received more than one-fourth of the doctorates in seven additional fields: library science, foreign languages, letters, psychology, area studies, education, and interdisciplinary studies. An interesting phenomenon is occurring in the "female" fields: As the degree level rises, so does the participation of men. An examination of the subfields under home economics, for example, showed increases for men in graduate study in family relations and child development and in foods and nutrition. Where did those men who earned 34 percent of the doctorates in home economics come from? Only 9 percent of the masters degrees and 4 percent of the bachelors's degrees in this field went to men. Unfortunately, the reverse phenomenon—an increase of women in "male" fields as the degree level rises—does not occur. At best, the proportion of women receiving master's degrees remained constant or increased slightly before dropping again at the doctoral level.

Even as graduate students, then, women remain concentrated within traditionally female fields. One wonders about their job prospects. Where did the 2,640 women with master's degrees in arts and letters find employment in

1974? Library science and education are fields with limited job openings. Currently, women may have a better chance for employment in traditionally male fields, where affirmative action has prompted a search for qualified women, than they do in female fields. Women must begin to explore a wider range of job possibilities.

Growth in graduate enrollments is expected to slow down in the period between 1974 and 1983. Projections indicate that women will earn almost twice as many of the first professional degrees in 1983-84, up from the current 9 percent to 17 percent. The expected growth in percentage of total master's and doctoral degrees earned by women is less impressive: an increase of 2 percentage points up 46 percent at the master's level and of 4 percentage points to 22 percent at the doctoral level (Simon and Frankel, 1975).

IMPACT OF PERSONAL AND BACKGROUND VARIABLES ON ACCESS

Before one can identify discriminatory practices, either individual or institutional, that result in differential educational access and attainment, one must examine the various processes and early experiences that shape a person and thus in part determine his/her educational decisions, progress, and ultimate attainment. People themselves are in large part responsible for what happens to them, in that they have come to perceive themselves in certain ways. They are aware of certain alternatives, consider certain options, and take certain actions that may lead to certain outcomes. For example, the underrepresentation of women in elite institutions of higher education may be attributable to failure to apply, which in turn may be attributable to the perception that they would not do well in such a setting. In this case, their underrepresentation can hardly be blamed on discriminatory institutional policies. Nonetheless, discrimination may be operating in the larger society to stifle women's opportunities and limit their options, a discrimination that makes itself felt early and in subtle ways. One's behavior is molded by a variety of factors, and it is these factors— including socialization, SES, aptitudes, ethnic and racial background, personal characteristics, self-image and expectations, and motivation—that affect participation and attainment.

EFFECTS OF SOCIOECONOMIC STATUS, ABILITY, AND RACE

Studies of the determinants of college entry and progress have found academic ability and school performance of prime importance. Sex and SES, defined in terms of parental income, occupation, and education, play significant roles as well. SES, however, is a confounding variable in that it correlates with achievement, personal traits and characteristics, interests, motivations, and values—all important influences in educational development.

The early analysis by J. S. Coleman and associates (1966) and the later work of C. Jencks and associates (1972) highlighted the differences in achievement among students of different SES and racial backgrounds. W. H. Sewell and R. M. Hauser (1975), in their intensive longitudinal study of Wisconsin high school students, provided critical information on the continuing role of SES and aptitudes in educational progress and achievement beyond high school. As early as 1957, Sewell examined the importance of social status to educational and occupational aspirations. In 1967, Sewell and V. P. Shah highlighted the differential impact of SES and of ability on educational and occupational development and status. Although both aptitude and past achievement affect postsecondary access and achievement, SES apparently exerts a stronger influence on girls than on boys, particularly at the lower levels. Girls of low SES are less likely to go to college than boys with similar aptitudes from the same low SES levels. Half the boys but only one-fourth of the girls in the highest ability but lowest SES quartile eventually attend college.

C. E. Werts (1968) reported differential SES effects for a highly able group (National Merit Scholars) of high school boys and girls. Bright girls from lower-class homes are significantly less likely to go to college than boys of similar backgrounds and abilities.

J. K. Folger, H. S. Astin, and A. E. Bayer (1970), in a study using Project TALENT data, observed differences in the effect of SES on the postsecondary plans of women and men. Consistent with Sewell and Shah's findings, low SES had a particularly adverse effect on college attendance of girls. Among high-ability, low-SES groups, only 52 percent of girls attend college, compared with 69 percent of boys. Assessing additional variables that might affect access to postsecondary education, the same study indicated that motivation, reflected in plans to attend college, and encouragement from parents and peers are important influences, independent of SES. Ability is equally significant for both sexes as a determinant of college entry but more important for men as a determinant of progress through college. For women, however, marital and family status assume an importance equal to that of ability as women progress through the educational system.

Using the same data source, Project TALENT, M. D. Brown (1974) found that the timing of plans to pursue postsecondary education significantly affects educational outcomes: Students who plan as early as the ninth grade to go to college are more likely to do so, whatever their ability and SES. Moreover, the effects of making early plans are stronger for girls than for boys. Brown also observed that, whereas high-achieving girls are as likely as high-achieving boys to pursue postsecondary education, girls of low SES, low ability or poor grades, or both are less likely to enroll in and pursue postsecondary education than similarly disadvantaged boys.

In addition, Brown found that both men and women are more likely to complete four or more years of college within five years if they have achieved in high school, come from high-SES backgrounds, taken a college preparatory program, and have plans in high school to complete at least four years of college.

Even though girls and boys do not differ significantly in achievement or SES, by the ninth grade fewer girls are taking college preparatory programs or planning to attend college. For instance, in 1960 only three in ten ninth-grade girls were in college preparatory programs, compared with four in ten boys; by twelfth grade, only 31 percent of the girls but 44 percent of the boys were in college preparatory programs. Further, only 32 percent of the ninth-grade girls but 43 percent of the ninth-grade boys planned to complete college; by twelfth grade, 28 percent of girls and 46 percent of boys planned on four years of college or more.

Brown concluded that girls whose high school achievement was poor suffered the greatest disadvantage in access to postsecondary education. Clearly, it is important for girls to make plans early to attend college and to enroll in the college preparatory track as early as the ninth grade.

Another study of the factors affecting college attendance found that high school rank is an important determinant for both men and women (Christensen, Melder and Weisbrod, 1972). Moreover, though parents' income and education are both important variables in predicting a man's college attendance, parental income has no significant influence on the college attendance of a woman, although father's occupation and parents' education do. Finally, having a college nearby significantly increases a woman's chances of college attendance but has no effect on a man's. Christensen and his associates concluded that if a man can pay the matriculation fees and meet the admissions requirements, he is likely to attend college. The probability that a woman will attend college, however, is profoundly affected by parental and community influences, as reflected in parents' education and values and in the availability of a college close to home.

The importance of SES in facilitating or hindering educational access and attainment should not be underestimated. Given two persons of equally high academic ability, the one from a lower socioeconomic background is less likely to attend a four-year institution, and this effect is particularly marked among women, whatever their race. SES seems to work to the advantage of men at the other end of the scale as well: Among students of low aptitude but high SES, the women (especially nonwhite women) are less likely to go to a four-year college. Finally, students of high SES, independent of ability, have high completion rates within each type of educational setting (noncollegiate institution, two- and four-year college).

INSTITUTIONAL PRACTICES

Clearly, men and women differ in their participation rates in high school programs, postsecondary institutions, graduate and professional schools, and fields of study. At each higher step of the educational system, fewer women participate. For example, in 1972-73, women constituted 51 percent of high school graduates; in 1973-74, they earned 45 percent of the baccalaureates, 44 percent of the master's degrees, and 19 percent of the doctorates (Grant and Lind, 1975).

In high school, slightly more boys are enrolled in college preparatory programs. Of the students enrolled in vocational-technical programs, girls are concentrated in business and office skills, whereas boys are clustered in trade and industrial areas. Girls graduate from high school with more preparation in foreign languages and English, and boys with more preparation in science and mathematics.

At the college level, women are more likely to attend small, less selective, less affluent institutions; they are disproportionately enrolled in Catholic four-year and private two-year colleges. Women are underrepresented at elite institutions and conspicuously absent from technical institutions.

The graduate and professional school enrollments of women lag behind those of men. A 1971 follow-up of the class of 1965 indicated that 56 percent of the women, but only 43 percent of the men, had taken no advanced study (El-Khawas and Bisconti, 1974).

Often the lower educational and occupational achievement of women is attributed to their internalization of the sex norms of society. If one accepts the notion that these norms are pervasive and that they are inculcated early, it becomes all too easy to say that nothing can be done by the time the student is in high school. An understanding of how the sexes develop in society should not be used to justify perpetuating inequities. Yet schools, colleges, and other educational institutions may be guilty of doing just that: Some institutional practices may have discriminatory consequences for women.

Admissions

Concern began to mount in the late 1960s that selective admissions policies at colleges and universities might penalize minority group members for their inadequate high school preparation. Two national conferences focused on barriers to higher education. One included a review of the impact of selective admissions on minority access and persistence by A. W. Astin (1970), who concluded that admissions practices based on high school grades and standardized test scores do indeed tend to exclude minorities. Since the dropout rates of black students attending white colleges are slightly lower than would be predicted from their high school grades and test scores, colleges can afford to introduce additional criteria to promote the admission of minority students without damaging their images or lowering their performance standards. Astin commented that higher educational institutions might better serve society if they aimed not at picking "winners" (those students whose abilities and past achievements virtually guaranteed that they would persist in college) but at admitting those students most likely to benefit from their programs. The second conference focused on open admissions with particular attention to admissions standards that penalize students from disadvantaged backgrounds (CEEB, 1971a).

These conferences centered on discrimination in the admission of minorities, but many of the same questions arise with respect to women: Do admissions standards and practices in higher education affect women adversely? If so, what aspects of the process have negative consequences, and in what ways are women affected? Unfortunately, no national statistics on the ratio of acceptances to applications exist to assess the extent to which women are discriminated against by not being accepted on the same basis as men. The review on rates of participation makes clear that women are disproportionately enrolled in certain types of institutions and programs, but to what extent that imbalance implies that other types of institutions reject women applicants is not known.

Pamela Roby (1973), confronted with the same lack of national statistics, has suggested that one might approach the situation somewhat differently to ascertain, though only partially, what is happening to produce lower participation and attainment rates among women. She observed that, since women graduate from high school with better grades than men and also make better grades in college, their lower participation in college and in graduate or professional schools could result from institutional policies to maintain higher standards for the admission of women than of men. Her solution is simply to admit more women, since women perform better. Roby does not deal, however, with applications and acceptances. That is, how many female high school graduates actually apply to college, and how many female college graduates apply to graduate or professional schools? The data on aspirations show that, at every level of the educational system, women have more modest aspirations than men. Perhaps, rather than relying solely on admissions procedures, postsecondary institutions should develop stronger recruitment programs to attract women.

In a study examining differential practices from bias in admissions, E. Walster, T. A. Cleary, and M. M. Clifford (1970) asked whether an applicant's race or sex affected the likelihood of his/her being admitted to college. They predicted that a black applicant of either sex would be preferred to a comparable white candidate and that, independent of race, men would be preferred to women. Identical applications, except for variations in the race, sex, and ability level, were submitted to 240 randomly selected institutions; acceptance or rejection constituted the dependent variable. All things being equal, men were more frequently accepted than women, particularly among students at lower ability levels. The authors concluded that women are more likely to be discriminated against in college admissions when they are of modest ability. Since more people of both sexes are of average or low ability, such discrimination penalizes women more often then men.

To learn whether women apply to as many different institutions as men, and whether they are accepted in equal proportions, data gathered from 1973 entering freshmen were analyzed. The proportions of men (20 percent) and of women (19 percent) applying to three or more colleges were about equal. Since 16 percent of each sex was accepted at three or more institutions, and since slightly fewer women submitted this many applications, women fared slightly better than men in terms of acceptances. Nevertheless, close to half of each sex applied to only one institution, and in this case, women did not do as well as men: 6 percent of men and 7 percent of women were rejected.

As noted earlier, women are not enrolled in selective institutions proportionate to their representation in the college population. To clarify this situation, 200 profiles of students from the fall 1975 entering freshman class were analyzed. The CIRP survey asked students to list the names of three other institutions to which they had applied and to indicate whether they had been accepted or rejected. Since students attending selective institutions are more likely to have applied to one or more institution, a sample of 20 selective institutions, including public and private universities and private four-year colleges, was analyzed. A random sample of 100 men and 100 women was selected from these 20 institutions; the only criterion for inclusion was that the student name three other institutions to which he/she had applied. Those institutions were coded by a selectivity index representing the mean Scholastic Achievement Test (SAT) score (mathematics and verbal combined) of all students attending that institution.

The 200 students in the sample had applied to about 233 different institutions. Very few had applied to institutions at the two lowest selectivity levels. Approximately equal numbers of men and women had applied to institutions at the top three levels; women applicants outnumbered men applicants at the first and third levels, and men outnumbered women at the second level. At each level, a higher proportion of women was accepted. This finding confirms, in part, the findings of Walster, Cleary, and Clifford (1970): highly able women (such as the women in this sample, who were enrolled in selective institutions) fare well in college admissions. If sex discrimination occurs, it is probably among less able students.

Another exploratory study was carried out to identify factors that are most important to students seeking admission to colleges and universities and to determine which factors operate differentially for men and women. Multiple regression analyses were carried out separately for each of four groups: white women ($N = 609$), white men ($N = 846$), nonwhite women (1,062), and nonwhite men (N = 991). All the students in the sample were under 30 years of age. The predictor variables included both student characteristics (from the 1973 CIRP survey) and relevant institutional characteristics. The dependent variables were (1) number of applications to college and (2) distance from home of the institution in which the student had enrolled. The premise was that women who applied to several colleges and who were willing to enroll in institutions some distance from their homes were also women willing to enlarge their options. The plan was to identify the characteristics of those women and to compare them with those of men, separately for white and nonwhite students.

The analyses revealed that white women who apply to four or more institutions differ from those who apply to fewer institutions in that they have higher degree aspirations, are more likely to come from Jewish backgrounds, and are younger. They are also more likely to plan on a career as a physician, to say that the opportunity for rapid advancement was a reason for choosing a career, to have liberal views about appropriate roles for women, and to have highly educated fathers.

In contrast, nonwhite women who make multiple applications are more likely to have highly educated mothers. Further, they tend to cite the availability of financial aid as an important reason for their choice of an institution, to choose selective institutions, to plan on a career as a physician, and to be unmarried and not dating.

Of the men who submit multiple applications, white men tend to come from Jewish backgrounds, to have highly educated mothers, to have high degree aspirations, and to enroll in predominantly male, selective, affluent institutions. Nonwhite men who submit multiple applications present a somewhat different picture: Like the whites, they tend to have high degree aspirations and highly educated mothers. In addition, however, they are distinguished from nonwhite men who do not make multiple applications by planning on careers that would enable them to contribute to society and by having liberal views about sex roles. They are likely to say that the advice of a counselor is an important factor in their choice of a college, as is the availability of financial aid (also true of nonwhite women submitting multiple applications). They plan to work while in college and feel that they may have to drop out temporarily because of financial constraints. In short, they emerge as highly motivated, liberal, and socially concerned students who face financial problems but have ways of dealing with them.

For the second dependent variable—attendance at a college away from home—distance between home and college was assessed on a scale of 5 miles or less to more than 500 miles. The greater the distance of their college from home, the more likely white college women were to report that they had been accepted at more than one college, that their fathers are well educated, that they have high degree aspirations, and that they come from other than a Catholic background.

In addition, they cited intrinsic interest as a motive in their career decision, and the reputation of the college as an important reason for their choice. Nonwhite women attending colleges far from home were likely to report that both their parents are well educated, that they plan careers in the arts, and that they give high priority to the life goal of influencing social values. They frequently express financial concerns and indicate that the availability of financial aid is an important consideration in their college choice.

The impression of the women, white and nonwhite, who apply to a number of colleges and enroll in a college distant from their homes is that they are highly motivated and career oriented. Finances obviously create problems for nonwhite women in this group, which is not surprising, since they are living away from home and attending relatively selective institutions. The analyses did not allow for causal inferences: That is, it is impossible to say whether willingness to make multiple applications and to live away from home opens up options in college and career choice that these women might not otherwise have considered, or whether initially high degree aspirations and career plans give them greater freedom to move out and upward. Highly motivated women are, however, more independent and more willing to consider multiple alternatives, thus enlarging their opportunities.

Some have charged that the admissions criteria of higher educational institutions discriminate against women. Before such a charge can be substantiated or dismissed, it is necessary to know just which admissions criteria various institutions use, and to decide whether the application of those criteria excludes women. Information on admissions criteria provided by four technological institutes and four four-year colleges indicated that institutions either do not keep good records of applications and acceptances or are unwilling to reveal them. Nonetheless, it seems clear that the grades the student earns and the courses he/she takes in high school are important considerations in admissions. Since girls generally make better grades than boys, they have the advantage on the first criterion. But since they are usually poorly prepared in mathematics and sciences—courses that the technological institutes particularly emphasize—they are at a disadvantage on the second. Obviously, women are at a disadvantage in applying to technological institutions because of the strong emphasis placed on mathematics and science.

Additional information was available for the present study from interviews with admissions officers at 19 private liberal arts colleges. When asked if an applicant's sex was considered in the admission process, eleven officers said it was not. Two reported that, because of housing limitations, they took sex into consideration. Another reported that this had been the case with them in the past, before coed housing was introduced. One officer reported that the institution had always enrolled more men than women and that if, in the future, they were to accept a larger proportion of women, a decision might be made to hold a balance between the sexes. One college had guidelines that dictated a maximum male enrollment of 3,000 and a minimum female enrollment of 1,000; further, they considered applications separately for each sex. Another admissions officer reported that the college accepted the same proportion of male and female applicants and that more men than women applied. Of the three remaining institutions, one was single sex, one was attempting to recruit men, and one was recruiting women.

Housing limitations, the maintenance of a balance between the sexes, enrollment quotas, and proportional acceptances can all constitute discriminatory practices in cases where a large number of highly qualified women apply to an institution; some of them may be rejected in favor of less qualified men. Only one institution in the liberal arts college sample was taking the affirmative step of actively recruiting women.

A number of research studies have asked whether women are discriminated against in graduate and professional school admissions. For instance, P. J. Bickel, E. A. Hammel, and J. W. O'Connell (1975) observed that applicants fared best in departments that required preparation in mathematics, since there were fewer applications to such departments and thus a greater likelihood of acceptance. Relatively few women, however, apply to such departments; most apply to departments that have high application rates. Thus, women do suffer in admission to graduate study. The authors concluded that this differential pattern cannot necessarily be blamed on discriminatory institutional practices but could be the result of earlier socialization that produces differences in high school courses taken. The fields that women are prepared to enter tend to be overcrowded, to have low degree-completion rates, and to offer poor job prospects.

Retrospective studies of graduate students (NIH, 1968; Centra, 1974) and medical students (Campbell, 1973) indicate that women in these groups feel that they are discriminated against both in admissions and during training. The NIH report was based on a study of 1961 college graduates who went to graduate school. It revealed that women face three major obstacles to entry: financial difficulties, family responsibilities, and lack of available graduate programs. Women graduate students also cited a number of changes they felt would encourage more women to enter scientific and medical fields. These include allowing part-time training, providing day-care facilities or allowances, increasing training stipends, and giving greater recognition to women in these fields (NIH, 1968). Regarding graduate school experiences, 15 percent of women doctorates, compared with 5 percent of men, mentioned sex discrimination in admissions (Centra, 1974). M. A. Campbell's report on women in medical schools categorizes and documents discrimination, reporting that recruitment and admissions represent one form of discrimination experienced by women in medical schools.

In 1972, the Task Force on the Status of Women in Psychology (TFSWP, 1972) surveyed over 100 psychology departments to identify discriminatory practices against women students and faculty. Asked to indicate the criteria used to assess an applicant's motivation, most departments mentioned letters of recommendation as the most frequent. Yet much evidence suggests that letters of recommendation often contain sex-biased statements that may adversely affect a woman applicant's chances. For instance, one study of sexism in graduate admissions tallied sexist comments that implied a lower level of expectation for women ("it would be good for a woman" or "marriage may deter her"), and traits irrelevant to graduate study (physical attractiveness: "she is a tall blonde"; marital and family status: "she has no children to keep her preoccupied"). Only one of 85 letters of recommendation for male candidates contained what might be regarded as a sexist comment, compared with 11 of 38 letters of recommendation for women candidates (Lunneborg and Lillie, 1973).

Financial Aid

An institutional practice that is a significant factor in access and attainment in postsecondary institutions is the awarding of financial aid. The availability of financial aid may determine whether a high school student goes to college, as well as the kind of institution he/she selects. Once the student is enrolled, persistence may be affected by the type and amount of financial aid. Women, particularly minority women, are often seriously concerned over their ability to finance postsecondary education, so financial aid is particularly crucial for them.

Historically, education for men has been considered a virtual necessity, whereas education for women has been regarded as luxury or frivolity. In point of fact, statistics from the Women's Bureau of the U.S. Department of Labor (1972) gave the following picture in 1973: Of the nearly 35 million women in the labor force, 7.7 million were single; 6.3 million were divorced, separated, or widowed; 3.7 million had husbands whose 1972 incomes were below $5,000; and 3 million had husbands whose 1972 incomes were between $5,000 and $7,000. In short, most women work, not to fill their idle hours or to buy themselves luxuries, but for the same reason men work: to support themselves and their families. Yet women are concentrated in low-paying "female" fields.

Postsecondary education and training can provide women with skills and competencies that will increase their access to higher status fields and thus increase their earning power. As work becomes increasingly technical, and as fields that have traditionally employed women convert to automation, women without adequate advanced training will be unable to find employment. Postsecondary education not only prepares women for the world of work but also prevents the underutilization or loss of talented people with high potential.

Nonetheless, outmoded beliefs and attitudes persist, with the result that young women continue to underestimate their need for education, and families— particularly low-income families—continue to give precedence to educating their sons. Postsecondary education at all levels continues to ignore the needs of women and to formulate policies that favor men. This attitude can prevail in the awarding of financial aid.

SOURCES OF FINANCE

Young people typically draw on a variety of sources to finance their post-secondary education, including their parents, spouses, earnings and savings, student aid programs such as college work-study, scholarships, grants, loans, and GI benefits. In addition, the low- or no-tuition policies of some public institutions may be considered a kind of financial aid.

Parental aid, the financial source with the longest history, continues to be the major source for most students. According to A. W. Astin (1975):

> For nearly 65 percent of the white women, parental aid is a major source of support for their freshman undergraduate year, while only 16 percent received no parental support. For 47 percent of the men, parental aid is a major source, while for only 28 percent it is not. Blacks are somewhat less likely than whites to rely on parental aid: only 33 percent depend on parental aid for major freshman support (p. 6).

One implication of this greater reliance of women—at least white women—on their parents for financial support in postsecondary education is that it makes them more generally dependent on their parents and more vulnerable to parental pressures and wishes, and thus reinforces their passive, submissive role. A second implication is that women from low-income families are at a particular disadvantage. If they must rely chiefly on their parents because no alternative financial sources are available to them, they may not go to college, both because their parents do not have money to send them and because low-income families regard postsecondary education for their daughters as unimportant. With respect to impact, Astin (1975) found that, except for women from high-income families, parental support generally increases the student's chances of completing college.

Support from spouse is relevant for only a small proportion of undergraduates. If students who are married when they enter college (about 2 percent of each sex) receive major financial support from their spouses, however, their chances of dropping out are greatly reduced. If they receive minor support from their spouses, their dropout rates increase; they would be better off receiving no assistance from this source. If students get married while in college, assistance from their spouses, in whatever amount, increases persistence; generally, such students continue to rely on other sources for major support.

Earnings from employment and savings are another means by which students finance their postsecondary education, although these sources are generally more helpful to men than to women. According to W. Bengelsdorf (1974), women have fewer opportunities for employment during the school year or in the summer; and, if they do find jobs, they receive lower wages than men. U.S. Bureau of the Census (1975a) data show that 83 percent of high school boys age 16 and over expected to earn some money between July 1973 and June 1974, in contrast to 67 percent of high school girls. Furthermore, one-third of the girls expected to earn under $1,000, while only 15 percent of the boys expected such low earnings. Indeed, 38 percent expected to make $7,000 or more during the year, compared with only 18 percent of girls.

Work-study programs, a major component of federal financial aid policy since the Higher Education Act of 1965, affect relatively few students. Of 1968 freshmen followed up in 1972, 13 percent of women and 9 percent of men reported participating in federally sponsored work-study programs (A. W. Astin, 1975).

N. Friedman, L. W. Sanders, and J. Thompson (1975) found evidence of sex discrimination in work-study programs: Men were about twice as likely as women to hold high-level jobs regardless of their college class, major field, or grade average. Half the women had low-paying clerical jobs. Yet even when men and women were employed at similar jobs, men were usually paid more than women. Women students were more easily satisfied with their jobs, a finding that the investigators attributed to early socialization, which leads women to expect and to be satisfied with lower-status, lower-paying, typically "female" jobs. E. M. Westervelt (1975) confirmed the finding that women in college work-study programs get lower paying jobs and added that they generally get less help in finding employment. To document this latter statement, she cited a situation at the University of Chicago where, in 1969, 30 percent of women and 36 percent of men got help from faculty members in finding jobs and 64 percent of men, but only 49 percent of women, found jobs relevant to their major fields.

Participation in federal work-study programs seems to reduce the student's chances of dropping out, and this is particularly true among women, blacks, and middle-income students (A. W. Astin, 1975). Since they are less dependent on parents for financial support, middle-income women who participate in these programs may develop an increased sense of self-confidence and autonomy that strengthens their motivation and enhances their persistence.

Scholarships and Grants

Scholarships and grants are, to a lesser extent, associated with increased persistence (A. W. Astin, 1975), although the effects are confined chiefly to women from low-income families. The Basic Educational Opportunity Grant (BEOG) program, created in 1972 by federal legislation, was intended to guarantee each student a "financial floor" to meet college expenses. The requirement of a parental contribution for a BEOG can create insurmountable problems for women, whose parents see no value in educating their daughters and are thus unwilling to make the contribution. The effect is particularly severe for women from low-SES backgrounds.

Sex-restricted scholarships work to the disadvantage of women: "Sex-restricted awards available at men's colleges have exceeded both in numbers and amounts those available to women's colleges, largely because of the greater number, size, and wealth of the more prestigious men's colleges" (Westervelt, 1975, p. 14). Although many prestigious men's colleges have begun to admit women, the proportions are still small. A more de facto form of discrimination in scholarship awards results from the concentration of scholarship funds in "male" fields such as the hard sciences and engineering. Athletic scholarships represent another form of de facto discrimination in that they are far more readily available to men than to women.

Fellowships as well are more often awarded to men than to women: A survey of prestigious fellowship programs revealed that about 80 percent of the awards in nearly 70 of these programs went to men (Attwood, 1972). This situation results less from sex bias on the part of those making the awards, however, than from women's lower participation rates in the competition for fellowships.

E. M. Westervelt (1975) noted possible sex discrimination in awarding National Defense Education Act (NDEA) fellowships: She cited testimony before the Special Committee on Education of the House of Representatives in 1970 stating that, although women constituted one-third of the nation's graduate students in 1969, they received only 28 percent of the graduate awards under NDEA Title IV, and only 29 percent of the awards under NDEA Title VI.

Loans

Loans, particularly under the federally sponsored Guaranteed Student Loan (GSL) program and the National Direct Student Loan (NDSL) program, are an important source of funding for postsecondary education. Students who want to attend a high-cost institution or an institution away from home are particularly likely to borrow. According to the Carnegie Commission on Higher Education (CCHE), however, the two federal loan programs are underfunded, set too many limits on eligibility, allow insufficient repayment time, and have an unreasonable differential in interest rates—all of which discourages students from applying (CCHE, 1968; Wren, 1975). Moreover, as Richard J. Ramsden pointed out, these federal programs may not give sufficient consideration to the problems of the woman student: "An ever-increasing proportion of women are going on to college and to graduate school and are borrowing to do so, yet the work patterns and income patterns of women differ from those of men. Whether present loan programs reflect sufficiently these differences, as well as differences in the ability to repay, is doubtful" (ACE, 1975, p. 7).

In the past, banks have discriminated against women attempting to obtain commercial loans. The effects of recent legislation designed to prohibit such discrimination have yet to be felt.

The current federal emphasis on loans to finance college education may fail to allow for the reluctance of many students—and particularly women—to incur large debts. A ten-year follow-up study of 1961 freshmen (El-Khawas and Bisconti, 1974) showed that men are more likely than women to borrow for their undergraduate and graduate education, and twice as likely to take out loans of $4,000 or more (4 percent of men and 2 percent of women at the undergraduate level; 6 percent of men and 3 percent of women at the graduate level). Women faced with the prospect of earning money to repay a loan in a job market that discriminates against them may justifiably be unwilling to borrow heavily. Moreover, if they expect to spend some time out of the labor force raising a family after college graduation, they may be even less willing to take loans.

Military-Related Benefits

Military-related benefits are another type of aid that favors men. GI benefits are a source of support for about 6 percent of the male and 1 percent of the female undergraduates (A. W. Astin, 1975). The new volunteer army sets higher standards for women enlistees than for men. Thus women must be better qualified, rather than equally qualified, if they are to receive educational benefits under the GI Bill (Bengelsdorf, 1974). ROTC benefits are a source of financial aid for about 2 percent of the white male undergraduates and virtually none of the female undergraduates. Military academies are just beginning to admit small numbers of women applicants. Students relying on GI benefits are more likely to drop out, whereas those relying on ROTC stipends are more likely to persist.

Financing Graduate Study

During the first year of graduate study, women rely more on their own savings or on their husband's earnings for financing, whereas men rely more on support from parents or relatives. More men also receive support from fellowships, scholarships, traineeships, and assistantships. This last source is important in that having an assistantship—and particularly a research assistantship—increases a student's chances of completing graduate study because such an award usually involves working closely with a faculty member, which in turn encourages persistence and may pave the way to better career opportunities. A teaching assistantship does not have the same positive effects. That more men have research assistantships and more women teaching assistantships, then, becomes significant. This difference may work against women graduate students in the long run. It is not, however, necessarily attributable to sex bias; rather, it may be explained by women's concentration in fields where research assitant-ships are simply not available on any larger scale.

Access to graduate school involves not just enrolling in any graduate program but enrolling in the graduate program of one's first choice. When asked why they had not enrolled in their first-choice program, men are more likely to say that they have not been accepted and women to say that they have not received any financial aid (El-Khawas and Bisconti, 1974).

Perceived obstacles to graduate study differ somewhat for men and women. Men are more apt to cite financial problems and women to cite family obligations. Reasons for interrupting advanced study also differ by sex: Women are more apt to mention family responsibilities and financial problems, whereas men more often discontinue their studies because they experience academic difficulties or lose interest.

SUMMARY AND IMPLICATIONS FOR GUIDANCE AND COUNSELING

There are some notable differences between the sexes in high school. For instance, boys and girls are sharply segregated in vocational and technical programs. In academic programs, women make better high school grades than men, but fewer of them plan to attend graduate or professional school. Girls are underprepared in mathematics and science even though those who enroll in these subjects do better work than boys. Among the reasons for not continuing their education after high school graduation, more women than men indicate that their plans do not require any more schooling. An examination of the relative importance of factors assigned to a student's selection of a particular college reveals that economic considerations are somewhat more important for women. Although the absolute number of women in institutions of higher education just about doubled between 1964 and 1973, the proportion of women still lags behind that of men.

A critical question relating to equal access is the types of institutions attended by various groups of students. Women attend smaller, less selective, and less affluent institutions. Women are also underrepresented in technological institutions. While in college, almost one-third of women are still planning to pursue careers in education and nonmedical health fields.

With respect to degree attainment, in 1973-74 women earned 45 percent of the bachelor's degrees, 9 percent of the first professional degrees, 44 percent of the master's degrees, and 19 percent of the doctorates.

Although aptitude and past achievement are important in post-secondary access and achievement, SES appears to exert a stronger influence on women than on men. Girls of low SES are less likely to pursue a collegiate postsecondary education than boys with similar aptitudes from the same low SES levels.

For a man, meeting admissions requirements and having the ability to pay matriculation fees are important considerations in college attendance. A woman's probability of attending college is strongly affected by such variables as the education and values of her parents and the availability of a college in the community. Moreover, SES affects the sexes differently with respect to completion rates. Men of low SES and high aptitude are more likely than their female counterparts to complete their training.

While some knowledge of the differential participation and attainment rates of men and women and of the personal and background factors that inhibit women in pursuing postsecondary education is essential to an understanding of the problem of discrimination in access, perhaps more pertinent is some knowledge of the institutional practices, such as admissions and financial aid, that may act as barriers. These are, after all, more vulnerable to change.

Women are more likely to be discriminated against in college admissions when they come from lower ability levels. Since more students of both sexes are found at those levels, discrimination penalizes women more than it does men.

Examining the factors in college choice reveals that women who have the willingness and interest to make multiple college applications and who wish to enroll in a college at a considerable distance from home are career oriented and have high degree aspirations. They also tend to have highly educated parents. The highly motivated woman is more independent and open to alternative choices, thus enlarging her opportunities and increasing her chances of being accepted. An applicant's high school grades and courses are crucial in admissions decisions. Since girls usually make better high school grades than boys, girls have the advantage on this criterion. On the basis of high school courses, however, girls are usually at a disadvantage, particularly at technological institutions, which require strong preparation in math and science.

Overall, women fare well for admission to graduate school, except in the top-ranking schools, where more male than female applicants are accepted.

Students rely heavily on parental aid to finance their education; women rely more on this type of aid than men do. Earnings from employment and savings are another important financial source. Men are generally able to earn more than women; moreover, women have fewer opportunities for employment during high school and the summer and receive lower wages than men when they work.

A study of federal college work-study programs found evidence of sex discrimination in work placements: Regardless of class level, academic major, or grade average, men are twice as likely as women to hold high-level jobs. Even when men and women hold similar jobs, men are generally paid more than women.

The Basic Educational Opportunity Grants program requires an "expected family contribution" before the student can receive a grant, a stipulation that can penalize those women whose parents do not see the value of an education for their daughters.

Loans, another important source of finance for an education, are often difficult for women to obtain because of their presumed employment and income patterns.

With respect to financing graduate education, during the first year of study women rely more on family resources than men. Men, however, receive more support from scholarships, fellowships, and traineeships. Moreover, men are more likely to be awarded research assistantships and women teaching assistantships, a barrier of sorts, since working on a research project implies a closer relation with the mentor and is in itself a valuable experience, useful in later career development.

Whereas family responsibilities and financial hardships are most likely to cause women to interrupt graduate study, men are more likely to discontinue their studies because of lost interest and academic difficulties.

If women are to have the same occupational opportunities as men, steps must be taken by the secondary schools to ensure that they have the necessary preparation. In dealing with high school girls, counselors have a dual responsibility: to help them develop more realistic outlooks about their future lives and to provide practical and detailed information about the financial costs of an education and about sources of financial aid. Another step that should be taken at the curricular level is to introduce high school girls early to technical and scientific materials so their interest will be aroused and their sense of competency developed.

The rather limited participation of women in postsecondary education and their concentration in traditionally female fields results from socialization to appropriate roles and occupations for women. Sex-role stereotypes continue to operate as women make decisions about their future lives. To overcome these stereotypes, which have already taken their toll in high school, colleges and, in particular, technological institutions should develop affirmative programs for women. Such programs should include special efforts to recruit high school girls for tutorials and for remediation in mathematics and science once they have been admitted.

The cost of postsecondary education is perceived by many young women as a particular problem as they make decisions about their future. Once in a postsecondary institution, they continue to have special concerns about financing. The type and amount of financial aid available has been found to affect decisions about postsecondary education as well as persistence while in college or graduate school. Since young women in general are more likely than men to depend on their parents for support, those whose parents do not value education for their daughters as much as for their sons may need financial aid as much as or even more than the male students.

Work-study programs are an effective form of financial aid in that they encourage persistence. These programs should continue to admit women; efforts should be made to place women in jobs traditionally reserved for men. Work experiences in nontraditional areas will help women to develop new competencies and enlarge their options. In addition, women should be encouraged to work while in college, since such experiences will make them more independent, personally and financially. Financial independence may have additional benefits in that women will begin to view themselves as a critical part of the economy and as competent to become leaders.

In graduate school, women should be encouraged to compete for research assistantships, since this experience offers the additional benefits of further learning, more interaction with mentors, and future employment opportunities. Furthermore, women should be encouraged to apply for fellowships, and professors should be encouraged to nominate women in greater numbers.

Understanding the internal forces that act as psychological barriers as well as the institutional constraints reviewed thus far in Chapters 2 and 3 is essential to an assessment of how counselors and counseling might facilitate women's educational and career development. Counselors dedicated to broadening horizons for clients of both sexes have much work to do. Yet counselors are human and they, too, are victims of forces that prevent changes in their attitudes and inhibit counseling for nontraditional options.

As young women are affected by socialization, so are counselors products of their environment. The degree to which their training and role models shape their experience is reflected in their later behavior as counselors. Even if their training is strictly objective, if it does not alert counselors to the stereotypic assumptions they may make, it cannot counteract the counselors' socialization. Conversely, if their training is sex biased, it may compound the effect. In examining the training of counselors it is as important to assess the characteristics of their trainers as it is to examine the training material.

COUNSELING FACULTY

The new counselor, emerging from a graduate program, is strongly affected by interactions with instructors. The latter have an impact not only through the knowledge they transmit to their students, but also through their values and attitudes that are communicated, perhaps imperceptibly.

Demographic variables affect individual attitudes, particularly on sensitive topics such as race, sex, and the expectations of minority or women students. Some surmise that sex and possibly race of professors affect interaction between faculty and student. Many writers, advocating a greater proportion of women on university faculties, point to the importance of role models in professional socialization. E. Almquist and S. S. Angrist (1971) found that career-oriented women are more affected by faculty members than noncareer-oriented women. "Students do not become committed to a career field without some positive relationship with role models who display the skills, meet the demands, and consciously enjoy the pleasure to be obtained from that pursuit. The most readily available models for students are, first, their professors" (p. 8).

Clearly college professors have attitudes about a student that depend on the latter's race or sex (see Chapter 2). Two studies—K. C. Christensen and W. E. Sedlacek (1972) and L. G. Garman and W. T. Platt (1974)—indicated that male and female students are viewed in a stereotypic fashion. Given this information, the sex of those doing the training becomes an important consideration.

While women faculty will not necessarily provide less biased counseling courses, their experience as women, as women counselors, and as women faculty will undoubtedly affect the outlook on professional women that they will communicate to their students. Moreover, programs that hire women are more likely to be open to nonstereotypic ideas.

L. E. Haun (1974), a member of the American Personnel and Guidance Association (APGA) Commission for Women, has presented data on the sex distribution of counselor educators. The primary source is the *Counselor Education Directory, 1974* (Hollis and Wantz), which lists 94 percent of all counselor education institutions. Overall, 85 percent of counselor educators are men and a greater proportion of women than men faculty is found at the assistant professor level and below (49 percent and 32 percent, respectively). The proportion of women faculty employed is far smaller than the proportion of women earning doctorates in areas appropriate for counselor educators.

The APGA listed 39,000 active members in 1975. Designation of sex and race/ethnicity are optional on the membership blanks used for the annual survey of active members. Consequently, not all members complete those items. Of those designating sex, 49 percent are men and 52 percent are women. The Association for Counselor Education and Supervision (ACES), with 4,000 members, is a subdivision of APGA. Sixty-eight percent of that group indicated sex on the membership form. Of this group, 1,800 or 67 percent are men, and 900 or 33 percent are women. Over half the ACES members indicated race: 90 percent white, 10 percent black.

For an exploratory study, the Higher Education Research Institute (HERI) asked 100 counselor education programs for a list of faculty and required courses and an explanation of their training. Of the 26 programs that responded, 2 (8 percent) have a female department head. Of the 191 faculty, 158 (83 percent) are men.

If one accepts the premise that it is discriminatory for women to be underrepresented on the faculty, most programs are guilty of discrimination. Most are probably also guilty of perpetuating discrimination in that they do not provide role models for women students and may be passing on antiquated values and attitudes.

Curriculum

The courses taught to counselors-in-training also provide information about sex bias. The survey of graduate departments, despite the small return, permits an examination of the courses in a counseling curriculum. With one exception, all programs have rewritten their catalogs and other material descriptive of the curriculum to reflect sex neutrality of students and faculty. This revision is at least an effort to maintain sex fairness in recruiting students. Of the 26 programs, only one provides a course specifically on women as a special subpopulation.

B. O. Pressley (1974) conducted a survey of the guidance and counseling divisions of state departments of education. Information available to state departments of education includes courses taught in university counselor-training programs. Pressley's survey found a paucity of courses on counseling girls and women. Only 12 programs offer such courses, yet 75 percent recommend that courses in counseling girls and women be offered within counselor education curriculums. Finally, the National Longitudinal Study (NLS) indicated the kinds of counseling courses practicing counselors have taken. While almost all counselors have one or more courses in educational, personal, and vocational counseling, less than half have similar courses on counseling minority group members and only 23 percent have two or more courses on minorities. Undoubtedly, a miniscule number are exposed to a course on counseling women. Finally while a practicuum or internship is usually required for the degree, most counselors have no supervised experience in minority group counseling and, although data are not available, probably none in counseling women.

Textbooks

In 1972 the American Psychological Association (APA) formed a task force to examine sexism in graduate psychology. The focus soon narrowed to one aspect of graduate education: textbooks, specifically "whether, and if so, in what manner, there exist erroneous and harmful conceptions and representations of either sex" (Birk et al., 1974, p. 1). Thirteen of the most frequently used texts, covering clinical psychology, child development, and tests and measurement, were content analyzed. The task force concluded that both errors of omission and commission are frequent, representation of women scholars is limited, and women are less preferred as subjects of psychological research and as subject material. The texts show limited career roles for women, thereby restricting career options, and there is little discussion of sex roles or differences.

C. K. Tittle, K. McCarthy, and J. F. Steckler (1974), in surveying tests and measurement textbooks for test bias, found that most books mention the problem of women, although not always in great detail. For example, L. Tyler (1971) included a section on test fairness, and A. Anastasi (1968) considered sex differences in an analysis of group differences. R. L. Thorndike and E. Hagen (1971) discussed cultural influences on test scores. Finally, Thorndike (1971) noted the concern about fairness in tests for minority groups, but found a lack of evidence of discriminatory use of tests in prediction. He showed a lack of concern over test bias and refers to students, instructors, teachers, and test developers as male.

Eight books were used by more than one program among the 26 in the exploratory study. While this number is not sufficient for a methodologically perfect study, it does allow an examination of textbooks commonly used to train counselors. Three of the most frequently assigned texts were chosen for content analysis: *Fundamentals of Guidance* (Shertzer and Stone, 1971), *The Work of the Counselor* (Tyler, 1969), and *Group Counseling: A Developmental Approach* (Gazda, 1971). The three criteria for the content analysis closely paralleled some developed by the APA task force: (1) Proportion of content devoted to women and to men;* (2) citations;† (3) sex-associated descriptors.‡

While traditional English uses the masculine pronoun when sex is unknown or when either sex is meant, the effect of this practice must be questioned. For instance, the APA task force report (Birk et al., 1974) noted that it is difficult to know whether the writer using "he" or "men" is referring to specific men or "mankind." Is an author who refers to the physician as "he" doing so because a large proportion of physicians is male, or is the author using the generic "he"? The task force concluded that "perhaps . . . when 'she' is not included, 'she' is, indeed, not included." In any case, since sophisticated readers cannot tell whether "he" refers to an individual man or people in general, neither can less sophisticated readers. They may get the impression "that women are less important . . . that there are fewer women in the world" of work and, whether their impressions are conscious or not, they may be subliminally perceived and stored.

J. W. Schneider and S. L. Hacker (1973) asked college students to select pictures that would represent topical titles for a sociology textbook. Two forms were used. Five of the 13 labels on one form contained "man-linked" labels (for

---

*Every tenth page in each book was divided into half pages, which were counted. The number of half pages devoted to women in any context was tallied; the number devoted to men, including reference to masculine pronouns, was also tallied. The number of charts, pictures, and graphs referring to men, women, both, sex unspecified, and nonhuman subjects was counted.

† The references to women and to men in the subject index were tallied.

‡ Descriptors for men and women were listed, with even numbers of pages surveyed for both sexes. Sexist colloquialisms were noted.

example, "Urban Man," "Political Man," "Industrial Man"), while the other form contained "nonman-linked" labels ("Urban Life," "Political Behavior," "Industrial Life"). The use of generic "man" led 64 percent of students receiving man-linked labels to submit only pictures of men, whereas only half of those receiving neutral titles submitted only pictures of men. The use of the masculine throughout counseling textbooks may have repercussions on counselors-in-training.

In the content analysis of the three texts, Shertzer and Stone had 110 half pages surveyed. Of this number, 4 (4 percent) referred to women and 57 (52 percent) to men. The Tyler volume consisted of 48 half pages: 45 (94 percent) described men and 2 (4 percent) women. Gazda included 52 half pages: 19 (37 percent) referred to men and 6 (11 percent) to women.

These texts usually refer to women in stereotypic terms. In Shertzer and Stone, they are seen as high school girls who value dating, dancing, social success, physical beauty, enticing manners, and clothes, while men are seen as high school boys who value athletics and car ownership. Boys are described as channeled into science, language study, or engineering without learning about choices; girls are described as playing "school." Tyler's descriptions are more stereotypic. Women are students and clients, men are colleagues. Women are receptionists or secretaries, contemplating divorce and looking for career options, dependent or "desperately [needing] a man to love [them]." Men are trying to decide between medicine and engineering careers, or whether to choose a career in dentistry; they enter the military service as immature boys and emerge grown up.

Gazda is more egalitarian. He refers to both men and women as colleagues. Females, however, are also Girl Scouts, mothers, and insecure students, while males, endowed with free will, are group leaders. The graphs and citations also reflect sex bias. Shertzer and Stone have 26 graphs or pictures in the pages surveyed. Of these, 2 represent men only, 2 represent both sexes, 12 are unspecified, and 10 are nonhuman subjects. Tyler has 4 pictures, 1 of men and 3 unspecified, while Gazda has 26 charts, 4 of men, 8 of both sexes, 9 unspecified, and 5 nonhuman subjects. While the graphs by no means represent a predominance of men, not one represents women only. When women are represented, there are always men represented too. Each book has graphs of men only.

The subject indexes do not yield many topics that deal specifically with either sex, although when there are references to a particular sex, it is women. Two references to women are in Shertzer and Stone, one in Tyler. Possibly, the importance of highlighting women's experience in counseling materials is finally being understood.

J. Whiteley (1975), surveying guidance textbooks, found that guidance theory is based heavily on psychological theory, bringing with it sex bias. Assumptions about women are made without data. Most guidance textbooks do not refer to sex differences, men-women, boys, girls, sex roles, human development, adolescence, or personality theory. When problems of sex bias are presented, they are not deemed sufficiently important to accent or develop. The effect of a woman's employment and career on her marriage is explored less in the guidance than in the marriage literature. Most counseling theories assume a biological basis for sex differences, giving little or no thought to the culture as the source of sex-role behavior. The personality theories from which counseling theories are drawn largely ignore the importance of socialization in developing sex-role behavior. The theoretical assumption that the problem is within the individual rather than within the society becomes a further source of bias in theory. Women's vocational development and concerns are either ignored or treated as trivial corollaries to men's career development.

In spite of the obvious shortcomings of textbooks in current use in guidance and counseling, it is still possible to teach a sex-fair course. Such a course could survey issues of concern in counseling women and critically examine the textbooks available in the field.

CERTIFICATION

Not only the training process but also how the job is structured and whom the system allows into counseling ranks have implications for the effectiveness of counselors and their interactions with students.

States regulate entry into the counseling profession at the elementary and secondary levels by means of counseling certification (Woellner, 1974). At the postsecondary level, control is exercised by professional associations and sometimes by state licensing boards. Data on the requirements of the latter are unavailable. The professional associations (including APA and APGA) set standards for approval of graduate training programs that usually include a supervised internship and specified courses.

A content analysis of state requirements for counseling certification indicated that, of the 50 states and the District of Columbia, 28 require a master's and 15 a bachelor's degree. The remaining states either list no specific degree requirements or no specific overall certification requirements for counselors. Moreover, most states do not specify that the degree be in guidance and counseling or in student personnel work. In addition to degree requirements (sometimes instead of them), 31 states require a specific number of hours of professional education with the median 21. Twenty states also require a practicum or supervised internship. Thirty-two require a teaching certificate, and 16 specifically mention that the counseling candidate must complete a median of 2.5 years of successful teaching before he/she is eligible to be a counselor.

The teaching requirement may result in counselors who are selected by principals as a reward for faithful service, sent back to school for the required courses, and then allowed to counsel students. They may have neither the natural skill, inclination, nor empathy to do so. Since most secondary school principals are men, men may be selected more frequently than women to seek counseling certification.

PRACTITIONERS IN COUNSELING

In understanding the background that counselors bring into the counseling interaction, it is important to examine counselors' characteristics and the kinds of contacts that counselors have with students. These background variables of the counselor are discussed below. In the first section of Chapter 5, we begin to explore how counselors' characteristics affect the counseling process.

APGA's membership breakdown by sex, which shows 52 percent women among active members, is probably influenced by two divisions with inordinately large female populations. The American School Counselor's Association (ASCA), concerned with primary and secondary schools, boasts a membership of 60 percent women. The National Catholic Guidance Conference (NCGC) includes 52 percent women. Likewise, the Association for Nonwhite Concerns (ANC) is 60 percent women, probably due to a greater number of women professionals in the minority population. Except for these divisions, all others are more heavily represented by men. The Association for Counselor Education and Supervision has a 67 percent male membership, while the Association for Humanistic Education and Development (AHED) is 50 percent men (see Table 1). Except for the ANC, whose membership is 84 percent black, members of APGA divisions are overwhelmingly white. Overall, 88 percent of responding members are white, 11 percent black, and 1 percent other origins. Only 47 percent, however, indicated their racial membership. The majority membership of APGA divisions ranges from a high of 96 percent white in the NCGD to a low of 80 percent white in AHED.

Other tallies of professional associations indicated similar ratios. G. B. Gottsegen and M. G. Gottsegen (1973) reviewed the role of women in school psychology. Data from the National Association of School Psychologists' (NASP) membership for 1972 indicated that 48 percent of the members are women, yet few officials of the association are women. A 1973 tally of APA membership by division indicated that the division of school psychology has the second largest number of women members. A tally of two divisions listed in the APA membership directory, using first names to assign gender identification, revealed that the division of school psychology membership is 39 percent female, 61 percent male. This division probably encompasses counselors in the elementary and secondary schools. The division of counseling psychology, covering professionals in colleges and universities, has a much larger male representation: 82 percent male compared with 18 percent female. The tally was done for the overall membership and for the three membership categories separately (fellows, members,

TABLE 1

Membership of Professional Guidance Associations, by Sex and Ethnic Category

Association	Active Members	Sex		Ethnic Category		
		Men	Women	White	Black	Other
American Personnel and Guidance Association						
Number	39,000	13,000	14,000	16,000	2,000	200
Percent		48	52	88	11	1
American College Personnel Association						
Number	9,000	3,500	2,800	4,000	500	
Percent		56	44	89	11	
Association for Counselor Education and Supervision						
Number	4,000	1,800	900	1,800	200	
Percent		67	33	90	10	
National Vocational Guidance Association						
Number	9,700	3,500	2,800	4,000	350	
Percent		56	56	92	8	
Association for Humanistic Education and Development						
Number	650	200	200	200	50	+ others
Percent		50	50	80	20	
American School Counselors Association						
Number	14,000	4,000	6,000	6,000	500	
Percent		40	60	93	8	

American Rehabilitation Counselors					
Number	3,000	1,200	800	1,200	75
Percent		60	40	94	6
Association for Measurement and Evaluation in Guidance					
Number	2,100	900	500	900	75
Percent		64	36	92	8
National English Counselors Association					
Number	1,200	450	350	500	65
Percent		56	44	88	12
Association for Nonwhite Concerns					
Number	1,600	500	750	150	800
Percent		40	60	16	84
National Catholic Guidance Conference					
Number	1,000	275	300	350	16
Percent		48	52	96	4
Association for Specialists in Group Work					
Number	1,000	450	300	450	25
Percent		60	40	95	5
Public Offenders Counselors Association					
Number	175	80	50	85	6
Percent		62	38	93	7

Note: All percentages are based on the number of members specifying sex and/or race on their membership blank. The overall response to an item inquiring about sex was 69 percent; 47 percent of respondents indicated their race.

Source: Data were collected by Higher Education Research Institute staff in personal communications with the American Personnel and Guidance Association.

associates). While more men than women were fellows (the highest-prestige elective membership category), the difference in proportions was small for both divisions. A much larger population of women, however, does not have full membership in the divisions of school psychology or counseling psychology. Thus it seems that women are underrepresented in the professional organizations. A survey in May 1974 of guidance and counseling divisions of all state departments of education indicates that among elementary counselors 35 percent are men, 65 percent are women, and among secondary counselors 57 percent are men, 43 percent are women (Pressley, 1974).

These data on sex representation among secondary school counselors are supported by the NLS counselor questionnaire results, which indicated a 58 percent male and a 42 percent female response. The NLS questionnaire is distributed to two counselors from each of over 1,100 schools. The sample is chosen randomly from a roster compiled by school principals. The questions deal primarily with work loads, counseling practices, and facilities.

Breakdown of the NLS data by region showed that a definite majority of counselors in the northeast, north central, and western regions are men, while in the South there are about even numbers of counselors of both sexes.

When asked about their ethnic background, an overwhelming number describe themselves as white (93 percent). Five percent are black, and less than 2 percent are other than black or white. Schools with the largest percentage of black counselors are in the South, in large cities, or in low-income areas.

Half the counselors who responded to the NLS questionnaire have three to nine years of full-time experience, while about a quarter have worked full time less than three years, and a quarter ten or more years. While 29 percent have been at the same school between five and nine years, 44 percent have been there less than five years. Most counselors have experience in schools with minority students; in schools where the minority population is greater than 20 percent, less than a quarter have worked. Only 12 percent have worked in schools where English is not the primary language for many students.

What are secondary school counselors' main duties? Most counselors have a heavy load: 56 percent are assigned between 300 and 700 or more students (U.S. Dept. of HEW, 1974). The greatest percentage of working time is spent in direct student contact (46 percent). Eighteen percent of time is spent in consultation with parents and school personnel, 17 percent is devoted to clerical work, and 10 percent to outside activities.

In terms of hours spent counseling, differences vary by region. Over half the counselors in the Northeast spend more than 20 hours a week counseling students, while in the South only about 30 percent spend that much time. These differences may be due to the affluence of the school districts: in the poor districts in the South the counselors may be required to do many other things besides counsel students.

What kinds of issues do counselors discuss with their students? Most frequently they discuss college plans (22 percent of the time), personal and family problems (17 percent), and career or vocational guidance (16 percent). A great majority advises students on how to find jobs (93 percent), and helps them with summer jobs (79 percent) or with part-time jobs during the school year (80 percent).

SUMMARY AND IMPLICATIONS FOR GUIDANCE AND COUNSELING

A survey by L. E. Haun (1974) indicated that 85 percent of counselor educators are men and a greater proportion of female than male faculty is found at the assistant professor level and below. A far smaller proportion of women is employed in colleges than is earning doctorates in areas appropriate for counselor educators.

ACES membership data showed that 68 percent of the membership indicated sex on the membership form. Of this group, 1,800 (67 percent) are men, 900 (33 percent) are women. Over half the members of ACES indicated race: 90 percent white, 10 percent black.

A HERI survey of counselor education departments indicated that 2 of the 26 responding programs (8 percent) have a female department head. Of the 191 faculty teaching in those programs, 158 (83 percent) are men while 33 (17 percent) are women.

Textbooks used in training programs are often biased. A survey of graduate texts in psychology indicates that both errors of omission and commission are frequent. Representation of women scholars in texts is limited; women are less preferred as subjects of psychological research and as subject material in the books. Moreover, the texts show limited career roles associated with women, thereby restricting career options, and there is little discussion of sex differences or sex roles.

Test and measurement textbooks usually mention test bias, although not in great detail.

Three common counseling textbooks show bias in their coverage of women. In one book, 4 percent of the pages refer to women and 52 percent to men. Another volume has 94 percent of its pages describing men and 4 percent women. In a third book, 37 percent of the pages refer to men and 11 percent to women. The women in these texts are usually presented in stereotypic terms.

There is a paucity of courses on counseling girls and women. Only 12 programs in a nationwide survey (Pressley, 1974) offer such courses, yet 75 percent recommend that a course in counseling girls and women be offered.

Sex and race breakdowns of members of the counseling profession show that of those responding to an APGA membership survey, 52 percent are women and 48 percent men. Members of APGA divisions are overwhelmingly white. Women represent 48 percent of members of NASP, yet few officials of the association are women. APA's division of school psychology is 39 percent female, 61 percent male, while the division of counseling psychology is 82 percent male, a much larger male representation, and 18 percent female.

A survey of guidance and counseling divisions of all state departments of education showed that, among elementary counselors, 35 percent are men, 65 percent are women, and among secondary counselors, 57 percent are men, 43 percent are women (Pressley, 1974). Counselors responding to the NLS survey are 58 percent male and 42 percent female. When asked about their ethnic background, the majority (93 percent) describe themselves as white. Five percent are black, while less than 2 percent identify themselves as other than black or white. Among the 26 programs in the HERI survey, only one provides a course on women as a special subpopulation. Nonetheless, with one exception, all programs have rewritten their catalogs and other material descriptive of the course of study to reflect neutrality toward the sexes of students and faculty. At least this indicates an effort to maintain sex fairness in recruiting students.

Few counselors have taken courses on counseling minority group members, and most have no supervised experience with minority group counseling.

Counseling certification requirements include a teaching certificate (in 32 states) and several years of successful teaching (in 16 states). Successful teaching is required for counselors in the secondary schools.

The sparsity of female counselor educators indicates that more should be hired. Since many more women earn doctorates in areas appropriate for counselor educators than are hired in such positions, unavailable qualified women should not be an issue. Affirmative action must be practiced. Women are often hired at the assistant professor level and later not given tenure. The implications, aside from the obvious inequity, are that students see powerful male department heads and weak female assistant professors and conclude that women will never rise beyond a certain level. This may discourage female students from aspiring to higher educational and career levels.

To encourage more women to enter the profession, more female students should be actively recruited for graduate programs in counseling. In the high schools, students of both sexes and of minority status should be exposed to counseling as a job possibility.

Since there is no book on guidance and counseling that brings together female psychology and counseling, new materials for those now being trained must be developed, as well as materials for those who have already been trained. Textbooks in use today in graduate training must be carefully reviewed, with guidelines provided to or by the publisher. Neuter expressions or both masculine and feminine pronouns should be used as standard publishing practice.

Courses on counseling girls and women must be added to the counselor training curriculum. The likelihood that such courses will be well received is high, since most departments surveyed by B. O. Pressley (1974) indicated a desire for this type of course. Courses on minority students should also be encouraged. Supervision and field experience with both groups should be a requirement of the training program. All these courses and field experience should be required for counselor certification.

Researchers should gather information on minorities in the counseling field, particularly nonblack minority members. The recipients of services and the system also need to be studied. State departments should set standards for training that would include antibias regulations. Professional associations should adopt guidelines for training programs to eliminate sex bias. The APA, for example, could withhold approval from programs of school and counseling psychology if they failed to meet established guidelines. The APGA and other professional guidance associations could publish statements encouraging non-sexist training.

CHAPTER

5

THE COUNSELING
PROCESS

After examining the forces that have shaped both counselors and clients, it is possible to look directly at the counseling process for possible inequity. Optimally, sex bias in counseling interaction should be evaluated through observation. Since studies of counseling interaction are not readily available, however, one must infer what takes place from a knowledge of counselors' characteristics and attitudes and from the materials used in counseling.

COUNSELOR CHARACTERISTICS AND ATTITUDES

The race and sex of the counselor have implications for the counseling relationship and the attitudes of counselors toward the sexes. Many studies look at the effects of race independent of sex and at those of sex independent of race, an approach that results in data gaps. Where possible, studies that look at both factors are presented, but some studies of one factor only are also included.

Race and Sex

B. L. Backner (1970) and T. N. Ewing (1974), who investigated the impact of counselors' race on student satisfaction with counseling, both discounted the importance of counselor-client racial similarity. Backner conducted three studies of black and Puerto Rican students' attitudes toward ethnic similarity of their counselors. The first study indicated that sex and age are more important than race for this group when selecting a counselor, while the second showed that students prefer counselors of similar ethnic background, but tend to be dissatisfied with their effectiveness as counselors. The third study concluded that the only students who favor a counselor of their own ethnic background are those already working with a counselor of the same background. Black and Puerto Rican students feel that similarity of ethnic background "doesn't matter" (Backner).

Ewing (1974), who had both black and white students rate counselors of both races, found that black students rate both white and black counselors more favorably than do white students. Ratings of helpfulness differ for individual counselors but do not follow a racial line. Ewing found little support for his hypothesis that the counselor needs to have the same racial or ethnic background as the client. Nor is there any support for a second hypothesis of differential effectiveness among counselors in counseling students with different racial or ethnic backgrounds. Racial similarity is not the important dimension, but rather the experiences of the counselor and the human qualities of both counselor and client.

V. Y. Peoples and D. M. Dell (1975) reported no systematic effect of counselor's race on observers' ratings of counselor's level of activity. Nonetheless, level of activity is significant, as is counselor effect. Active counselors are perceived as more helpful and competent than passive counselors. The Peoples and Dell study suffers from a limited generalizability: Since only one counselor of each race is involved, it is impossible to know whether results are due to individual differences or to counselor race.

Other studies showed that black clients return in greater numbers to black counselors (Heffernon and Bruehl, 1971), that self-exploration for black students is greater with black counselors (Carkhuff and Pierce, 1967), and that black students give higher counselor effectiveness ratings to black counselors (Banks, Berenson, and Carkhuff, 1967; Gardner, 1972). None of these studies, however, measured the actual impact of the race of the counselor on client progress but only the client's perceptions of counseling effectiveness with counselors of the same or different race.

Studies of the effect of counselors' sex on the counseling interaction are considerably more disparate. Some show no significant relationship between sex and variables such as client satisfaction, various forms of counselor behavior, and counseling effectiveness. Others suggest that the relationship is interactive with status or experience.

M. Scher (1975) was interested in the relationship between verbal activity, sex of counselor and client, counselor experience, and perceived success of the counseling interaction. He used videotapes of selected counseling interviews to assess level of verbal activity and pen and pencil measures completed by both client and counselor to assess the outcome of counseling interaction. He concluded that sex neither of the counselor nor of the client is significantly related to therapeutic outcome. Female clients tend to talk more than male clients, but this does not affect the outcome. Only the experience of the counselor is significantly related to the outcome.

Another study, which investigated the relationship of client and counselor sex, experience of the counselor, and outcome of the interaction, found that inexperienced counselors of both sexes are more empathic and active and elicit more feeling when paired with same-sex clients (Hill, 1975). Experienced counselors of both sexes with a same-sex client focus more on feeling and are more empathic, while with an opposite-sex client they are more active and directive and do not focus on feeling. Hill showed that clients of women counselors report more satisfaction with their sessions than clients of male counselors, thereby somewhat contradicting Sher's finding.

L. Brooks (1973), interested in the relationship of self-disclosure to sex of client and counselor in a university setting, found that client-counselor pairs containing a female show greater self-disclosure than all-male dyads. In addition, females disclose more to male therapists, and males disclose more to female therapists. Males reveal more to high-status interviewers (Ph.D.-level counselors), while females reveal more to low-status interviewers (counselors-in-training). Finally, high-status male interviewers elicit more self disclosure from all clients than do low-status males, but status does not make any difference with female counselors.

That counselor status is an important dimension, particularly as it interacts with sex, is supported by A. B. Heilbrun, Jr. (1971), who is interested in determining under which conditions women are most likely to drop out of therapy or counseling situations. After ascertaining clients' level of readiness for counseling, he found that those at a low level prefer greater directiveness from men than from women therapists. When the counselor's status is low, however, low-readiness subjects prefer less directiveness from men than from women. With a high-status therapist, high-readiness women prefer less directive interviewers. A knowledge of the client's readiness for counseling and of the counselor's status and amount of directiveness can lead to better counselor-client pairs and to smaller dropout rates.

J. Mezzano (1971), investigating attitudes of secondary school youngsters toward counselors of both sexes, found that boys in every grade prefer male counselors, except in dealing with issues of home and family. Girls shift toward preference for male counselors as they get older. This increasing preference for male counselors may indicate that men have greater prestige in society.

C. A. Carter (1971) found advantages in being a female therapist, arguing that women are socialized to display qualities necessary in any therapeutic interaction. These include empathy, warmth, and "natural" interviewing abilities. Male therapists-in-training must be resocialized to display these characteristics. She thinks there are several types of clients for whom women are better therapists than men, such as female hysterics, psychotic patients, female delinquents, and women experiencing developmental crises. Extrapolating from the latter two cases, female counselors might be most skilled with female behavior problems in the schools and possibly with men, as well as women, who are experiencing developmental crises.

Counselor Attitudes

Another characteristic of the counselor that affects the interaction is his/her attitude toward clients of both sexes. Could the knowledge of a person's sex affect the educational and occupational expectations, evaluations, and treatment by a counselor?

Research findings are contradictory. In a now classic investigation, I. K. Broverman et al. (1970) found that mental health clinicians hold a double standard for a mentally healthy man and woman, and that these views parallel sex-role stereotypes. While the adult and masculine concepts of mental health are not much different, the adult and feminine portraits of mental health are quite different. A. Maslin and J. L. Davis (1975), studying sex-role stereotyping among counselors-in-training, indicated that counselors-to-be are similar to Broverman's earlier sample of clinicians. Both men and women view healthy adults and healthy males in approximately the same fashion. Women expect healthy women to be the same as healthy men or healthy adults, whereas men expected healthy women to be more stereotypically feminine. The women's movement may account for the great congruity of female subjects' responses.

C. R. Brown and M. L. Hellinger (1975) concluded that a majority of therapists have ambivalent attitudes toward women. Nonetheless, female therapists have more contemporary attitudes toward women than male therapists, and therapists with less experience are more traditional in their views toward women.

W. W. Friedersdorf (1970) also found sex bias on the part of counselors: Male counselors perceive college-bound girls as destined for traditional feminine occupations at the semiskilled level, whereas female counselors perceive college-bound girls as interested in college-level occupations. S. I. Abramowitz et al. (1975) reported that women aspiring to medical school are judged more sternly by morally traditional than by liberal counselors. Traditional counselors consider that the psychoeducational history of female clients shows less psychological adjustment than that of male clients. A. M. Collins and W. E. Sedlacek (1974) showed that college counselors perceive differently the reason for which male and female clients initiate counseling. Men are seen as more likely to have vocational-educational problems, while women are seen as having emotional and social problems.

In vocational counseling, A. H. Thomas and N. R. Stewart (1971) found that women with deviate (traditionally masculine) career goals are not as highly approved by counselors as women with conforming goals. Women with "inappropriate" career goals are seen as needing further counseling. The link with experience persists again here, although this time it is the inexperienced women counselors who are more accepting, while inexperienced men are least accepting. Experienced counselors of both sexes are equally accepting.

N. K. Schlossberg and J. J. Pietrofesa (1974) argued that counselors and clinicians hold stereotypes that are no different from those of the general population and that, regardless of sex, they are biased against women's entering male fields. They propose a training model to eliminate counseling bias that includes lectures and readings to raise the counselors' consciousness about women's roles, consciousness-raising sessions, audio and video role playing that emphasizes sex roles, and participation in developing special programs for women. In an earlier study, the authors found that a coached female client expressing ambivalence about a masculine career field is, in 81 percent of the cases, encouraged not to pursue this area.

Other studies present a somewhat different picture. W. C. Bingham and E. W. House (1973a) found that in general counselors express more positive than negative attitudes toward women and work, although more men than women indicate negative attitudes. In another study by the same authors (1973b), male counselors are less accurately informed than female counselors about the abilities and occupational alternatives available to women clients. The authors concluded that female counselors may be more clear, positive, and supportive of women clients.

M. L. Smith (1974) found no evidence that sex or ethnic group has any effect on counselors' evaluation of academic potential, and that this is true for both male and female counselors. Variables much more potent than sex, such as institutions chosen, aptitude, achievement, and personal traits of women, affect predictions of success. Finally, Hill et al. (1977) argue that counselor-client gender pairings do not yield simple results. Their findings indicate "that counselors' reactions to female clients vary according to problem type, counselor sex and client age, which suggests that women should not be used as a general simple category in research" (pp. 64-65). That women are lumped as a group in all the research described above may account for the contradictory findings.

COUNSELING MATERIALS

Early in the century, vocational counseling consisted of disseminating information. An individual with the proper amount of information about careers and jobs was thought capable of making a rational decision about the future. Today the belief prevails that such decisions cannot be made without objective information about the individual's assets and limitations. Therefore, tests and instruments have been introduced.

Tests and Instruments

Counselors often rely on tests to provide a more complete picture of the individual and to facilitate the collection of information and the exploration of alternatives. The five major types of tests are general mental ability, specific aptitude, achievement, interest, and personality tests.

Beginning in the mid-1960s, an awareness of the cultural bias of many tests in common use began to manifest itself. Many psychometricians now agree that tests do not function in the same way for minority group members as for middle-class whites. Research has looked at tests overall, considering their applicability to the criteria they must meet. Until recently, there was little research that scanned each test item individually for bias, thereby permitting an understanding of whether sex as well as racial bias might exist in many tests.

According to the College Entrance Examination Board (CEEB), every year 6.5 million achievement tests are used for selection and placement. This number is likely to increase. That tests may have a great effect on the life of the test taker is underscored by a study (Goslin, 1967, cited in C. K. Tittle, K. McCarthy, and J. F. Steckler, 1974): Teachers tend to view standardized tests as an accurate measure of potential, and achievement tests as important determinants of subsequent academic success.

According to the National Institute of Education (NIE) (1975) guidelines for assessing sex bias in testing, bias may occur in tests at three levels: in the inventory itself, in the technical information, or in the interpretive information.

The Tittle, McCarthy, and Steckler study was done to determine whether bias arises in selecting items for tests, whether it is mainly a function of language usage such as generic pronouns, or whether it is a combination of both. An analysis of language usage in nine achievement test batteries indicated that all but one use more male than female nouns and pronouns. The tests are the California Achievement Tests, the Comparative Guidance and Placement Program, the Iowa Tests of Basic Skills, the Iowa Tests of Educational Development, the Metropolitan Achievement Tests, the Sequential Tests of Educational Progress, the Science Research Associates Achievement Series, the Stanford Early School Achievement Test, and the Stanford Achievement Test. A sex-role stereotyping analysis of the same materials showed women portrayed exclusively as homemakers or in pursuit of hobbies. Young girls carry out female chores. In professional representation, some items imply that the majority of professions are closed to women and that teachers are women while professors, doctors, and company presidents are men. Tittle, McCarthy, and Steckler concluded that most tests contain numerous sex-role stereotypes. They also cautioned against possible discrimination against women in the development and use of educational tests in that these may reinforce sex-role stereotypes and restrict individual choice.

M. F. Tanney (1975), in reviewing literature on the impact of test language, found no studies on the effect of the linguistic structure of items on test results. She noted that criticisms of the empirical development of interest inventories are much more damning.

Most frequently critiqued in recent years are interest inventories. Several educators (Prediger, 1972; Holland, 1974; D'Costa, 1969) have claimed that interest inventories have multifold value. For the student they facilitate vocational exploration and broaden career choices; for the counselor they are a vehicle to understand student needs. Birk (1975) and others questioned whether interest inventories in their present form and usage provide a broadening and effective experience for women, or whether socioeconomic status (SES) and demographic variables are more powerful in determining a student's choices.

Interest Inventories

Tittle, McCarthy, and Steckler (1974) argued that several developers of interest inventories construct their tests on an empirical basis with little theoretical formulation to guide them. The empirical approach is also criticized for being based on the world as it is—a man's occupational world. This basis limits women's choices by limiting their occupational scales on several inventories and by reflecting the cultural stereotypes on others without questioning what this means for vocational counseling of women. The assumption is implicit that what is is equivalent to what should be.

Three widely used interest inventories are the Strong Vocational Interest Blank (SVIB) and its successor, the Strong-Campbell Interest Inventory (SCII); the Kuder Occupational Interest Survey (KVIS); and Holland's Self-Directed Search (SDS).

Strong Vocational Interest Blank

The Strong Vocational Interest Blank, revised in 1966, has two forms, one for men and one for women. While many counselors have given both forms to women, this procedure is expensive and time-consuming. Moreover, male clients rarely, if ever, have been given both forms. C. B. Johansson and L. W. Harmon (1972) reported that giving both forms to a single client can lead to erroneous interpretations. Since the development of the SVIB did not control for sexual-stereotypic differences, taking the form for the opposite sex may depress scores on a given scale, because the test taker rejects the sexual-stereotypic items. The scores obtained are largely unpredictable. For example, Johansson (1975) noted that 67 percent of a given sample of women respond "like" to the occupation of interior decorator, compared with only 28 percent of men. This response is unusual for a man and similar to that of a criterion group of actors. A woman who responds "like" to that scale is indicating little that is unique to her gender. Johansson argued that good items can be written for both men and women by not referring to gender, but the problem of different response patterns by sex remains. A corollary problem is whether men and women in the same occupations have different interests. One way around this response set lies in the construction of the scales. Whereas a woman who takes the male form of the SVIB has her scores compared with those of men in general rather than with those of a same-sex group, scales can be developed that compare male scores with a male criterion group and female scores with a female criterion group. N. S. Cole (1972) argued, however, that there is enough similarity between the sexes in interest structure that generalizations beyond the status quo of an inventory are possible in exploring new career opportunities for both. Johansson concluded that it is necessary to report scores for all available scales and, when possible, to base them on appropriate sex norms.

C. M. Huth (1973), in a review of recent studies using the SVIB women's form, pointed to an apparent bipolar split between traditional and nontraditional careers, arguing that the SVIB does not predict which women will become "career committed." D. P. Campbell (1973) suggested that this failure to differentiate women's interests is due to an inadequate understanding of the role of vocational interests in the career development of women. He noted that the career-homemaker dichotomy is unproductive and obscures individual differences within each group, differences important for counseling. J. M. Birk (1974) said that research that identifies a dimension of career conflict, such as homemaker versus career, could stimulate counselors to explore areas during counseling which would be broadening to women clients.

Minority women have even greater problems with interest inventories. J. P. Gump and L. W. Rivers (1975) argued that interest inventories are of little practical value by themselves, yet when used with aptitude and achievement patterns, they can help certain students select a career pattern. They questioned whether minority women fit this category. Interest data pertaining to black women are scarce; the only study, using an early version of the SVIB, showed that response among black women on the interest scale for nurses equals that of a criterion group of white nurses. Gump and Rivers criticized the revised SVIB for not reporting criterion data for black women for any occupation. Consequently, the black woman who takes the SVIB has her responses compared with those of whites. Since the background experiences of the minority woman force her to develop different interests from those developed by white men and women, Gump and Rivers argued that a mismatch of interests will result. Both the predictor (the inventory) and the criterion (the reference group) are biased against the minority woman. Harmon (1970) and R. P. Anderson and G. Lawlis (1972) also pointed to significantly different patterns of response on the SVIB for disadvantaged women.

Numerous counselors pointed to the manual and handbook as further sources of race and sex bias. Test administrators usually become familiar with the instrument through the manual, which provides a description, guidelines for usage, and data about scale construction and validation. The test administrator will probably read the manual to administer the inventory and interpret results in a standardized way.

Birk (1974) looked at the manuals of four interest inventories, noting that in varying degrees the materials contain both explicit suggestions and subtle implications that could effect women negatively. For example, Birk (1975) cited a passage from the SVIB manual: "Many young women do not have strong occupational interests, and they may score high only in certain 'premarital' occupations. . . . In such cases, the selection of an area of training or an occupation should probably be based on practical considerations—fields that can be pursued part-time are easily resumed after periods of nonemployment, and are readily available in different locales" (Campbell, 1966, p. 13). This advice may indeed be taken to heart by guidance counselors. Birk recommended changes: (1) Develop a writing style that does not bias in favor of the masculine; (2) use case studies that represent and portray both sexes equally in nonstereotypic roles; (3) challenge the status quo by stating the right of all individuals to the full range of career options; and (4) caution the test administrator about any limitations of options provided by the inventory and suggest ways to counteract these limitations.

Birk (1975) found that the options for women in the SVIB manual are limited and that the status quo of women's roles is accepted throughout. She noted that the reader of a 1969 supplement could easily forget that a woman's form of the SVIB exists, since the opening sentence is: "Men in different jobs have different interests." This sets the tone for the supplement, which uses the masculine pronoun throughout. Birk concluded that the manual must be revised to eliminate the impression that only men are worth discussing.

Related to bias in the manual is bias in the interest inventory instructions often provided in the manual. That instructions can affect the results of the inventory was supported by H. S. Farmer and M. J. Bohn (1970), who administered the women's form of the SVIB to 25 married and 25 single women. Results indicated that, under instructions meant to reduce the level of home-career conflict, scores of career scales (author, artist, psychologist, lawyer, physician, life insurance sales) increased significantly and scores of homemaker scales (buyer, business education teacher, secretary, office worker, elementary school teacher, housewife, home economics teacher, dietician) decreased significantly over scores received under standard instructions.

Strong-Campbell Interest Inventory

D. P. Campbell (1973), agreeing with many critics, said that the SVIB "does tend to perpetuate stereotypic roles of men and women, at the expense of women, both by the kinds of items included . . . and the kind of information provided on the profile." He also concurred that the "statistics of 'What has been' should not be blindly followed to create 'What will be.'" At the time of these statements, Campbell was revising the SVIB and entitled the revision the Strong-Campbell Interest Inventory (also known as the unisex Strong). The SCII is an improvement over the SVIB:

1. It eliminates the obvious bias of asking men and women different questions by combining items into one booklet.

2. It modifies the vocabulary to eliminate references to gender, except where gender is an integral feature of the word, in which case both versions are listed (for example, actor/actress).

3. It eliminates dated items, American-culture-bound items, and weak items.

Tittle, McCarthy, and Steckler (1974) still found some problems with the scale, in that a number of occupations on the profile carry an "m" (male) and no equivalent "f" (female). This could still make it appear to women that occupations are viewed as male even though women receive a score for them.

M. C. Whitton (1975), reporting on the reliability and validity of the SCII, showed that for male subjects, male and female occupational scales are equally good predictors of career possibilities. For female subjects, female occupational scales yield a higher (although not significantly higher) percentage of possible career choices. There appears to be a large gain in the percentage of career choices that results from consideration of all occupational scales rather than just same-sex scales. These findings reinforce the view that all subjects should receive scores on all occupational scales.

Kuder Occupational Interest Survey

The Kuder Occupational Interest Survey, Form DD, intended for college-bound subjects, also comes under scrutiny. The KOIS consists of 100 forced-choice items. The results indicate the similarity of the person's interest to the interest of satisfied subjects for a variety of occupations and college majors (the criterion scale). Sixty occupation-based scales and 30 college-major-based scales are reported for the inventory. In the latest KOIS, male and female subjects responded to the same items, yet they are treated separately during the scale development. Scores are reported for both based on both-sex criterion groups.

Most criticism of wording and restrictions on women's choices that were relevant to the SVIB apply as well to the KOIS. The separate criterion groups of males and females again suggest that sex differences are important in occupations and in measuring interests. C. B. Johansson and L. W. Harmon (1972) suggested that good scales could be built by combining males and females in an occupation and comparing their item responses with those of a combined reference group. In a study reported in the 1966 manual, Kuder found a high correlation between scores based on male and female criterion samples and those based on three samples of women. Therefore, reporting of scores for females based on male criterion samples is a valid procedure for representing their interests in fields where there are opportunities for women, but criterion data are unavailable. If a woman enters a traditionally male field, she will be more satisfied if her interests resemble those of men in the occupation. Kuder, in the KOIS interpretive leaflet, considers it important to emphasize scores based on the subject's own sex and to use opposite-sex criterion scales for added insight into a subject's interests. If the highest scores are obtained on opposite-sex criterion scales, then this may indicate that good career options are not presented by same-sex scales.

Birk (1975) noted that the earlier version of the KOIS uses masculine pronouns throughout. She also pointed out that women's occupations and college-major scales are eliminated from male profiles, but that women's profiles have rankings from both male and female scales. She wondered on what basis this procedure was adopted, noting that if this is not empirically validated, it should be so stated. She concluded that this version of the KOIS seems to accept the status quo.

Tittle, McCarthy, and Steckler (1974) concentrated on bias in the earlier KOIS' interpretive leaflet, still in use, noting that the distinct status of women is reinforced by separate occupational and college-major scales. Examples given in the leaflet, such as the occupational profile of "Maxine Faulkner," do not allow for a woman with interests in both a traditionally male field and male college majors. While the new leaflet does make a change in this respect, the older leaflet will probably continue to have an impact on test takers and counselors.

Tanney (1975) noted that the new KOIS and its new leaflet are improved. The new KOIS is generally free from gender-linked items, although a few do sneak in here and there. No longer are test takers required to state whether they have ever engaged in or dislike particular activities, but instead are asked to indicate their preferences. This question neutralizes the effect of socialization on test takers and focuses on their opportunities to engage in various activities.

Holland's Self-Directed Search

Holland's Self-Directed Search (SDS)—self-administered, self-scored, and self-interpreted—included several different types of items: occupational daydreams, liked and disliked activities, competencies, and occupational preferences. Criticism of the SDS followed lines similar to that leveled at SVIB and KOIS.

One alleged problem is that the SDS is biased in its handling of interests and abilities, since women have not had sufficient opportunity to develop interests and abilities in some areas because career options are predicated on past experiences, which in the test are divided largely along sex lines. In a recent study, G. D. Gottfredson and J. L. Holland (1975) found that the activities rating is the least efficient predictor of future choice for women, while the competencies rating is least efficient for men. Tanney (1975) pointed out that activities listed under the "realistic" heading are those to which males are exposed in manual arts classes, while females have only limited exposure. Conversely, "conventional" (typing, office work) activities are probably experienced more frequently by females. Since the response categories are "like" or "dislike or never done," low scores on the "realistic" or "conventional" scales have different meanings, depending on the sex of the test taker. Others have pointed to the sexist language in occupational titles.

Birk (1975) also criticized the SDS manual, noting that it focuses on male users and takers: The manual accepts the status quo without an explanation that men tend to get one kind of score more frequently while women tend to get another. Birk pointed out that the SDS instructions are problematic. The SDS compares the test taker's initial daydream occupation with a summary code. For the man or woman with nonsetereotypic occupational daydreams, this may lead to discrepant codes. How the counselor deals with this discrepancy must be carefully examined. Counselors may assume that the summary code is the more accurate of the two and thus encourage the explanation of stereotypic occupations for a client who initially had different goals.

Suggested Guidelines

Test bias has been quite well documented. Movement has occurred to revise some of the inventories. While the changes are not sufficient in many instances, there are proposals for further remedies. The National Institute of Education guidelines (1975) proposed the following to eliminate bias in testing:

1. In the inventory itself: (a) The same form should be used for women and men unless it is empirically shown that separate forms minimize bias. (b) Scores should be given on all occupations for both women and men. (c) Item pools should reflect experiences and activities equally familiar to both sexes. If this is impossible, there should be a balance of activities familiar to each sex. (d) Occupational titles should be in gender-neutral terms, or both male and female titles should be present. (e) Use of the generic "he" should be eliminated.

2. In the technical information: (a) Sex composition of criterion and norm groups should be included in the description of these groups. (b) Criterion and norm data should be updated every five years. (c) The validity of interest inventories for minority groups should be investigated.

3. In the interpretive information: (a) Interpretive materials should point out that vocational interests and choices of men and women are influenced by many environmental and cultural factors. (b) The user's manual should state that

all jobs are appropriate for qualified people of either sex and should attempt to dispel myths about women and men based on stereotypes.

Concerning minority test-takers, Gump and Rivers (1975) suggested the following guidelines: (1) Efforts to eliminate bias should be aimed as strenuously toward members of minority groups as toward whites. (2) Interest inventories should be administered early to minority women to present a larger array of occupations, since black women traditionally make early career decisions with a limited choice of occupations. (3) Student handbooks should include accurate information about proportions of minority men and women in various occupational roles. (4) Counselors should encourage minority students' consideration of broad occupational choices even when the number of minority-group members in given roles is low. (5) Publishers should establish response rates on homogeneous scales for minority men and women. (6) Normative groups for occupational scales should include minority groups. If so, their response patterns should be compared with the majority and item modification made where necessary. (7) New inventories appropriate for use with minority women should be developed.

Finally, innovative vocational counseling techniques are suggested. For instance, C. R. Dewey (1974) suggested a new instrument, the Non-Sexist Vocational Card Sort (NSVCS), developed because of bias in traditional tests. Seventy-six occupations from the SVIB and the KOIS are typed on three-by-five-inch cards and coded according to Holland's six personality types. Occupations are chosen to represent a wide range of vocational values. Clients of both sexes sort the NSVCS cards into three piles: "would not choose," "in question," and "might choose." They then sort the "would not choose" cards according to why they are not chosen. The clients' comments are recorded. The same step is followed with the "might choose" group. Finally, clients are asked if they feel that any occupational areas are omitted from the 76 cards. If other occupations are mentioned, they are related to vocations already in the hierarchy. Dewey pointed out that it is difficult for any test to be completely nonsexist while using a language that is biased, but the NSVCS provides a process-oriented approach that gives a greater range of vocational choices to both sexes.

The technique focuses on individual differences rather than on differences by sex. According to Dewey, the technique is less sex-biased because the same vocational alternatives are offered to both sexes, the gender of occupational titles is neutralized, and the process orientation of the technique allows the counselor and the client to confront and explore sex-role biases as they emerge in the counseling session.

Other Counseling Materials

College Admissions Manuals

College admissions manuals address themselves overwhelmingly to male individuals (Tittle, McCarthy, and Steckler, 1974). The American College Testing Program *Counselor's Handbook (1972-73)* (ACT, 1972a) mixes usage, referring to the student as "he" or "his/her"; however, it is inconsistent. For the most part the sample reports and profiles that illustrate the materials are of male cases. *Using ACT on Campus (1972-73)* (ACT, 1972b) refers to both the item writer and the student as "he." All sample profiles and examples are male. Finally, the *Comparative Guidance and Placement Program* of the College Entrance Examination Board (CEEB, 1971b) refers consistently to counselor, faculty advisors, and students as male.

The same use of masculine and feminine word forms that appears in textbooks used to train counselors (see Chapter 4) also appears in the college admissions manuals. In a study highlighting the impact of the referent's sex on career materials, R. Plost (1976) presented two unfamiliar occupations to 600 students in a slide-tape presentation. One occupation was depicted by a female model, the other by a male. Results indicated that both sexes prefer occupations presented by a same-sex model, underlining the importance of eliminating the generic "he" and of providing appropriate sex models for career and guidance materials.

Occupational Handbooks and Materials

Although information on contents of career guidance materials is scarce, several studies have focused on illustrations in career materials. J. M. Birk, J. Cooper, and M. F. Tanney (1973, 1975) found that women are underrepresented in both the 1972 and 1974 *Occupational Outlook Handbook (OOH)* compared with their numbers in the labor force, while members of ethnic minority groups are slightly overrepresented. Overall, there is little change between the two editions. There is overrepresentation in illustrations of one sex at the expense of the other.

Birk, Cooper, and Tanney concluded that career illustrations do not accurately portray the presence of women and minorities in occupations. The illustrations may convey subtle but pervasive impressions of sex- and race-appropriate career aspirations. Occasionally, women and some minorities are portrayed in nontraditional areas, but men are too rarely shown in similar nontraditional occupations.

These findings are important in view of the popularity of *OOH*. Over 80,000 copies of the 1972-73 edition were distributed to high school, college, and educational guidance centers. Birk, Cooper, and Tanney asserted that these illustrations may limit the horizons of the women (and men) who use the *OOH.*

They recommended that counselors specifically counter the possible deleterious effects of these materials. For example, at the counseling center where two of the authors are employed, a notice is posted over career guidance materials warning about the possible bias of the materials, but assuring clients that counselors will attempt to make all options "explorable."

A study by L. Vetter (1975) of different career guidance materials included student materials in the *Vocational Guidance Quarterly*'s career literature bibliography with publication dates of 1970 or later, and two bibliographies of commercial and noncommercial materials.

Like the Birk, Cooper, and Tanney studies (1973, 1975), Vetter's analysis showed a disproportionate number of illustrations of men: 61 percent men, 21 percent women, and 18 percent both.

An exploratory study conducted by the Higher Education Research Institute (HERI) at six Los Angeles metropolitan area high schools looks at the contents of high schools' college libraries. The schools, chosen for ethnic and socioeconomic representation, include two predominantly white middle- and upper-middle-class schools, one racially balanced middle-class school, one middle-class black school, one lower-class black school, and one predominantly Chicano lower-class school. The intent of the study was to find out what information is available in the schools in the absence of data on the content of guidance libraries.

HERI compiled lists of the most commonly available college reference materials, college guides, financial aid and scholarship information, and career and vocational materials. These include about 20 general college guides (such as *Barron's*), 10 references to financial aid, and 6 general references in the college library, and 10 sets of career pamphlets, 35 general references, and 21 community college and vocational school catalogs in the career library. Overall, the reference materials schools include in both their college and career libraries vary widely. Most schools depend on free materials because funds for other materials are unavailable. Two career counselors at inner-city high schools stressed that although audiovisual aids and information were needed to contact a broader population of students, the cost of such materials and equipment was prohibitive. Another career counselor, agreeing that audiovisual aids are useful, found that film strips present only stereotypic options. In all, the contents of these libraries were quite limited.

Another original study conducted for this project was a content analysis of the 1974-75 *Encyclopedia of Careers and Vocational Guidance* (*ECVG*) and the *OOH*, which yielded similar findings. Pictures of men only overrepresent their number in the labor force, while illustrations of women only greatly underrepresent their participation. Only 11 percent of *ECVG* and 17 percent of *OOH* illustrations represent women only, compared with their representation of 39 percent in the labor force. Another 14 percent of pictures in *ECVG* and 10 percent in *OOH* represent both sexes. Blacks are underrepresented in *ECVG*

TABLE 2

Content Analysis of Illustrations by Sex, *Occupational Outlook Handbook, 1974–75,*
Encyclopedia of Careers and Vocational Guidance, 1974–75
(in percent)

	Occupational Outlook Handbook			Encyclopedia of Careers and Vocational Guidance		
Category	Men	Women		Category	Men	Women
Age (N = 113, 26)				Age (N = 223, 37)		
Young	19	46		Young	13	35
Middle age	73	54		Middle age	82	59
Old	8	0		Old	5	5
Affect (N = 127, 37)				Affect (N = 253, 44)		
Smiling	6	3		Smiling	4	9
Sad	2	3		Sad	<1	0
None	92	94		None	95	91
Activity level (N = 124, 27)				Activity level (N = 251, 38)		
Active	8	4		Active	23	16
Passive	92	96		Passive	77	84
Type of activity (N = 139, 35)				Type of activity (N = 265, 51)		
Helping	17	34		Helping	19	45
Nonhelping	83	66		Nonhelping	81	55
Person(s) being helped (N = 24, 12)				Person(s) being helped (N = 50, 23)		
Men	71	8		Men	60	39
Women	21	83		Women	24	52
Both	8	8		Both	16	9

Source: M. Harway, H. S. Astin, J. M. Suhr, and J. M. Whiteley, "Sex Discrimination in Guidance and Counseling," report for the National Center for Educational Statistics, U.S. Department of Health, Education, and Welfare (Washington, D.C.: Government Printing Office, 1976).

89

(3 percent, compared with 11 percent in the labor force), but somewhat over-represented in *OOH* (18 percent).

The *ECVG* was also analyzed for other variables. Women in illustrations are young more often than men (35 percent, compared with 13 percent). While most illustrations are expressionless, of those that convey affect, over twice as many women are smiling. A much larger proportion of women is in helping positions (45 percent, compared with 19 percent men). These three findings support the belief that women are often stereotypically represented as helpful, pleasant, and attractive.

The *OOH* results were parallel: More women than men are young (46 percent and 19 percent respectively) and helping (36 percent and 17 percent respectively). In contrast to earlier findings, however, fewer women than men are smiling or passive (see Table 2).

Institutional Catalogs

College and vocational school catalogs comprise a major portion of materials in guidance and counseling offices, especially at the high school level. Catalog information affects students' perceptions of the academic environment they are about to enter. Since no studies deal specifically with catalogs, a content analysis was conducted for a random sample of 100 colleges and 19 proprietary schools in the third and final original study. Half pages were tallied for each catalog and a percentage calculated for the half pages devoted to men (including the use of the masculine pronoun) and those devoted to women (Table 3). Tabulations were separate for two- and four-year institutions and proprietary schools. Tallies for single-sex colleges are not reported here.

Illustrations, photographs by sex, and departmental descriptions were also tabulated. Items descriptive of an environment favorable to women, such as special services for women students, extension or nondegree programs, women's studies, and women's athletic programs, were noted.

Overall, a far greater proportion of catalog content is devoted to men than to women. Four-year colleges and universities show the greatest disparity in their treatment of the sexes; 23 percent of half pages are devoted to men, less than 1 percent to women. The other content refers to "he/she," "you," or to neither sex. In catalogs for two-year institutions, 16 percent of the half pages are devoted to men and 2 percent to women. Proprietary catalogs provide the most equitable treatment: 14 percent men, 9 percent women.

Proprietary schools provide fewer special services for women than two- and four-year colleges, perhaps because they provide fewer student services in general and have few programs for any specific population. Colleges themselves do not frequently mention special services for women. Only 2 percent of four-year institutions and 11 percent of two-year colleges mention women's centers. Six percent of four-year colleges have gynecologists, while no two-year college

TABLE 3

Content Analysis of Text in Institutional Catalogs
(in percent)

Category	Four-year Institutions (N = 3,124)*	Two-year Institutions (N = 468)*	Proprietary Institutions (N = 238)*
Text devoted to men	23	16	14
Text devoted to women	<1	2	9
Catalogs including:			
Affirmative action statements (AAS)	64	66	43
"Sex" in AAS	46	22	21
"Age" in AAS	13	–	7
Catalogs mentioning:			
Women's resource center	2	11	–
Gynecological services	6	–	–
Day/child care	2	11	–
Men's varsity teams	52	55	–
Women's varsity teams	26	22	–
Women's studies	6	11	–
Degree in women's P.E.	49	44	–

*Number of half pages.
Source: Harway, et al., op. cit. (see Table 2).

catalog mentions this service. Two percent of four-year colleges and 11 percent of two-year institutions have child care, and 6 percent of four-year and 11 percent of two-year colleges have a women's studies curriculum. Twice as many catalogs mention male as female varsity teams, while about half the colleges mention a degree in women's physical education. While materials descriptive of departmental offerings do not unanimously specify the sex of students, those that do mention men (the range is from 12 percent male mentions in psychology to 43 percent in education). No department mentions women specifically.

The catalog illustrations (Table 4) treat men somewhat differently from women. Overall, more than one-third of the illustrations in all three types of institutional catalogs represents men only. Twenty-five percent of illustrations in four-year catalogs and 29 percent in two-year catalogs represent women only. The largest proportion of illustrations in proprietary catalogs represents women (45 percent). When illustrations are broken down by type or location of activity, some striking patterns emerge: In four-year catalogs women are almost never

TABLE 4

Content Analysis of Illustrations in Institutional Catalogs

Category of Illustrations (by Sex)	Four-year Institutions $(N = 3,124)^*$	Two-year Institutions $(N = 468)^*$	Proprietary Institutions $(N = 238)^*$
Percentage of men only	37	38	34
Percentage of women only	25	29	45
Percentage of men and women	37	33	22
Science labs			
Men	42	50	50
Women	6	–	50
Both	52	50	–
Business (secretarial labs)			
Men	21	20	–
Women	29	20	78
Both	50	60	22
Auto/technical labs			
Men	60	100	100
Women	10	–	–
Both	30	–	–
Computer work			
Men	58	20	–
Women	8	40	100
Both	33	40	–
Home economics			
Men	–	–	–
Women	80	–	–
Both	20	–	100
Radio station, photography			
Men	78	50	100
Women	22	50	–
Both	–	–	–
Contact sports (football, hockey, soccer, basketball, baseball)			
Men	68	100	100
Women	4	–	–
Both	28	–	–
Dance, other sports, exercise class			
Men	–	–	–
Women	67	100	100
Both	33	–	–
Professors			
Men	59	100	50
Women	5	–	10
Both	36	–	40

TABLE 4 (Continued)

Category of Illustrations (by Sex)	Four-year Institutions $(N = 3,124)^*$	Two-year Institutions $(N = 468)^*$	Proprietary Institutions $(N = 238)^*$
Administrators			
Men	100	—	83
Women	—	—	17
Both	—	—	—
Electronics, drafting			
Men	40	100	50
Women	—	—	50
Both	60	—	—
Nursing			
Men	—	—	50
Women	60	100	50
Both	40	—	—
Child care, food service			
Men	27	33	100
Women	60	33	—
Both	13	33	—

* Number of half pages.
Source: Harway, et al., op. cit. (See Table 2).

illustrated in technical labs, while men are infrequently shown in nursing pictures. Men are almost always the only sex pictured in contact sports, while women are most frequently pictured alone in dance or exercise activities. Professors and administrators are usually men.

While most institutions have an affirmative action statement in their catalogs (69 percent of four-year, 66 percent of two-year, and 43 percent of proprieatary institutions), and some mention sex specifically (46 percent, 22 percent, and 21 percent respectively), few programs specifically meet the needs of women. Except for the proprietary schools, few role models for women are provided either in faculty ranks or in administration. What impact these catalogs have on students can only be surmised. The limited vistas for women shown in this literature may convince many high school students that the options for women are indeed limited in postsecondary education.

SUMMARY AND IMPLICATIONS FOR
GUIDANCE AND COUNSELING

Race and sex affect counselor behavior and the attitudes that counselors hold toward the two sexes. Most studies showed that counselor-client race similarity is not the important dimension, bur rather the experience of the counselor and the human qualities of both counselor and client. Similarly, neither the sex of the counselor nor the client is significantly related to therapeutic outcome or to counseling effectiveness. Only the experience of the counselor is significantly related to the outcome.

In terms of attitudes, most mental health professionals are either negative or ambivalent toward women. Mental health clinicians, who have a double standard of mental health, hold different concepts of what constitutes a mentally healthy man and woman. These concepts parallel sex-role stereotypes. Most therapists have ambivalent attitudes toward women; however, female therapists have more contemporary attitudes toward women than male therapists. Counselors with less experience are often more traditional in their views toward women.

The tests, materials, and theories used by practicing counselors comprise perhaps the most concrete and best documented area showing bias. Among the overall findings:

1. Educational tests may reinforce sex-role stereotypes and restrict individual choice.

2. An analysis of nine achievement test batteries indicated that all but one use a higher frequency of male than female nouns and pronouns. A sex-role stereotyping analysis of these materials showed women portrayed exclusively as homemakers or in pursuit of hobbies. Some items imply that the majority of professions are closed to women.

3. Test developers have based their instruments on the world as it is—a man's occupational world. This basis limits the choices for women by limiting their occupational scales on several inventories and by reflecting the cultural stereotypes of women on others without questioning what this means to the vocational counseling of women. The assumption is implicit that what is is equivalent to what should be.

Several interest inventories show indications of sex bias:

1. Numerous counselors have pointed to manuals and handbooks as further sources of race and sex bias. Bias in the interest inventory instructions that are provided in the manual can also affect the results of the inventory.

2. Many college admissions manuals are biased, addressing themselves overwhelmingly to male individuals.

3. Content analysis of illustrations in career materials showed that such materials overwhelmingly stereotype the sexes.

College catalogs are also aimed primarily at men, with far greater proportions of content devoted to men than to women.

Because counselors generally have stereotypic attitudes toward women who behave in nontraditional ways, women who do not conform to the norm, whether by choosing careers in engineering, choosing not to marry, or displaying traditionally masculine qualities such as assertiveness, may meet with resistance from their counselors. Therefore, all counselors need to examine their attitudes toward women so that they do not unfairly discourage women from nontraditional life styles. The schools must provide consciousness-raising sessions for their staffs specifically designed to combat sex-stereotypic attitudes.

While current research indicates that counselors hold stereotypic attitudes toward the sexes, the impact of these attitudes on counseling and guidance activities is not clear. Future research should clarify the interrelationship of counselor attitudes and counselor behavior.

Several groups are already refining tests and career guidance materials, but change is slow to come. Tests and materials may not be modified much in the near future.

In the interim, it is the counselors' responsibility to raise questions about every tool they use, whether it is an interest inventory, a career brochure, a college catalog, or the *OOH*. They must ask whether the information or the test reflects stereotypic roles for men and women, and whether the materials tend to close certain career options for either sex. They must take steps to counteract the stereotypic assumption of any materials. The counselor and the client must confront and explore sex-role biases as they emerge in counseling sessions and pursue avenues that are broadening rather than binding.

CHAPTER

6

RESULTS OF
COUNSELING

What impact do different kinds of counselor behavior and counseling programs have on the student-client? Unfortunately, this impact is most difficult to document. The two primary questions that counselors need to answer are: "Are we helping?" and "How can we improve counselor effectiveness?" (Pine, 1975).

One problem in counseling evaluations is that different criteria are used to evaluate effectiveness. In some cases it may be an increase in grade point average, in others improvement in reading skill, in still others intelligence test scores. One person can evaluate counseling with one criterion and conclude that it has been reasonably successful, while another person with a different criterion can come to the opposite conclusion. The use of different criteria has implications for sex bias. For instance, "adjustment" may be viewed as the desired result of counseling for women while "actualization" is the goal for men.

B. Shertzer and S. C. Stone (1971) noted other difficulties in evaluation: Most counselors have no time, no training in evaluation, inadequate measurement devices, and incomplete school data.

B. R. Lasser (1975) suggested that evaluation become part of the counseling process as "outcome-based counseling," focusing on the attainment of specific goals for the client. The process would concentrate on the consequences of counseling rather than goals and procedures as ends in themselves.

There are two direct sources of information about the effectiveness of counseling: student reports and counselor or institution reports. Student reports reveal who uses which counseling services and their degree of satisfaction. Counselors' or institutions' reports explain the counseling services and also reveal usage. The data that follow are presented separately by sex when possible.

STUDENT REPORTS

Students' reports of their counseling experiences are necessarily colored by their perceptions of the effectiveness of the interaction. Reports about the kind and extent of contact with counselors for the most part are nonevaluative.

High School Students

High school students participating in the National Longitudinal Study were asked to name the individuals with whom they had frequently discussed post-high school plans. Parents and friends are most often singled out, with females slightly more likely to turn to them. Guidance counselors are likely to be sought by only about one-fifth of students of both sexes. Again, females are slightly more likely to seek counselors. Of all ethnic groups, blacks are somewhat more likely to confer with a guidance counselor over future plans, although again the numbers are relatively small.

Men and women have similar perceptions about the counseling services available to them in high school, although women more often think the school provides ideas about their work and employment counseling. Blacks and Hispanics more often than whites agree that their school provides counseling for further education, employment, and personal problems.

How do high school students feel about their counseling experiences? Most students completing the NLS (over 80 percent) think that they can see a counselor when they need to. This is true across sex and ethnic groups, and most (about 80 percent) think that guidance counselors usually have the information they need. In terms of content of the counseling interaction, then, most students seem satisfied. When asked to rate the overall excellence of the guidance and counseling program, a majority still appears satisfied, but the percentage declines for all groups to just over 60 percent, and less than 33 percent are satisfied with the job placement services.

A follow-up study of Los Angeles high school students one year after graduation (Los Angeles Unified School District, 1975) provided data about student satisfaction with counseling experiences. A majority of graduates (59 percent) thinks that the high school counseling staff is friendly and accessible, but only 45 percent think that the advice on post-high school education is worthwhile. Minority students are more satisfied with the advice than whites, but there are few differences between the sexes. There is some consensus (66 percent) that teachers and counselors are more interested in the college-bound than in the employment-bound student. While men and women agree on this issue, more minority than white students also agree. A majority of students across all groups agrees that the school staff has little time to discuss academic or personal problems with them.

Students at the University of Pittsburgh were surveyed when they were freshmen, seniors, and graduate students on satisfaction with the counseling they received in high school (Jones, 1973). Less than one-third think that high school counseling suits the students' needs. White males are most satisfied, black females least satisfied. Only 4 percent, however, think that the counselor is prejudiced toward blacks or women or deals with them in a stereotypic manner.

When queried about the influence the counselor has on career choice, most students (80 percent) report "no influence," although whites more often than blacks tend to report "no influence." Nearly two-thirds think that the counselor has never tried to discourage students from pursuing a career in a field in which they express interest. Blacks are more likely to believe the opposite is true, and white women are more likely than white men to agree with the blacks. Only one-third agree with the career advice given by the counselor: 17 percent report that the counselor talked about a wide range of career opportunities. One-half of the students think that the counselor knowingly fails to discuss possibilities in certain careers because of sex. Again, the counselors' sex bias seems to demonstrate itself in terms of omissions rather than commissions.

College Students

What are college students' perceptions of their college counseling experience? Few sources answer this question. Consequently, the Higher Education Research Institute (HERI) asked 100 college alumni offices to send any alumni survey that might deal with satisfaction with counseling experiences. Results were disappointing: Most colleges have no such survey, and those that conduct alumni surveys ask questions outside the focus of this study. Only one study at Michigan State University provided a limited picture of the role of counseling in college, and this picture is not reported for each sex separately. For instance, respondents indicated what effect a number of persons or events have upon their career plans or decisions during college. The four sources of advice ranked lowest are, in order: academic advisor, vocational testing program, psychologist or vocational counselor, and job placement center. When asked to rate 17 different sources on help getting a job, respondents again rated counseling services rather low. The job placement literature ranks seventh, followed by personnel of the center; the academic advisor is eleventh, and the counseling center fourteenth.

In a follow-up study of two cohorts of college freshmen (freshmen in 1961 and 1966) and the influence of others on their career choices, A. S. Bisconti (1975) found that spouses are the most influential advisors. Less than half of 1 percent of respondents indicated that college placement personnel are "most influential," and only 4 percent of the 1961 and 10 percent of the 1966 cohorts recall using the placement center. Eight percent of the 1966 freshmen, however, obtained their current job through the college placement office, indicating an 80 percent success rate for this counseling service.

K. C. Christensen and T. M. Magoon (1974) asked a sample of 85 female and 85 male college students to rank-order sources of emotional and educational-vocational help. Friends and parents are considered first for help with emotional problems, while faculty, friends, and parents are first for help with educational-vocational problems. Counselors rank lower for both problems.

One can conclude from these findings that college students are not less satisfied with the counseling services available to them than are high school students, but that they make less use of these services. It appears that in many colleges, students are not even aware of the counseling resources, especially for personal problems.

COUNSELOR AND INSTITUTIONAL STUDIES OF IMPACT

Two kinds of data can be compiled by counselors for the services they provide: statistics on who utilizes the services and information on the impact of the services.

High School Counseling

At the high school level, both kinds of data are sketchy. Traditionally, high school counselors have been too preoccupied with myriad tasks to keep good records or to follow up their counseling. An exploratory study conducted by HERI at six Los Angeles high schools of varying ethnic and socioeconomic levels verified this situation. Counselors queried about their students' post-high school plans have few data on graduating students and become defensive over any request for data. Where some data are available, counselors think they are inadequate. Although they think information should be improved, counselors have little hope for better data because of inadequate time for collection. The available data vary widely in type and quality; counselors also are not uniformly interested in collecting this information.

College-Level Counseling

At the college level, documentation on individuals who use the campus counseling services is just beginning. Every student is not automatically assigned to a counselor (except an academic advisor) at the college level, as is done in high school. In fact, the student often must seek the services. Thus, keeping records on who is and is not utilizing the services becomes important.

W. H. Sharp and B. A. Kirk (1974), in an attempt to identify which students seek counseling and at what point in their college career they do so, found that counseling initiation is greatest just after school begins and declines over time. Women tend to initiate counseling earlier in the academic year. Men who seek counseling during final exams are least like the average student and need the most counseling. D. W. Sue and B. A. Kirk (1975) provide demographic data on clients using university counseling services, specifically on the frequency of Asian-American versus non-Asian use of the services. They find that a proportionately greater number of Asian Americans than the general student population uses the counseling center, but they underutilize psychiatric services. Chinese-American females are the highest users of mental health services (50 percent), while Japanese-American and non-Asian females do not differ significantly in their use.

M. S. Perez (1975), looking at Mexican-American students' attitudes toward counseling services, found that only 17 percent have ever used the services. Counselors of the same sex and ethnic background are preferred by these students and by a control group of white students. Initial complaints are about stresses caused by the financial and academic demands of the university. Female students experience more stress over security and inclusion in the university community. Overall, Perez concluded that Mexican-American students are less positive about therapy and counseling and have less confidence in mental health workers than nonminority students.

Some university counseling centers are developing materials on the effectiveness of their services and on their clientele. A data bank of 176 institutions' counseling centers has been compiled at the University of Maryland Counseling Center with 103 institutions stating (in 1974-75) that they had such materials. Specific data are not available at this time.

Some preliminary tabulations from the University of California, Los Angeles, give some sense of who frequents a university counseling center. These data, for the academic year 1974-75, indicate that a great majority of clients is female (62 percent). Initial problems vary: For females, the most frequent problems deal with career issues, followed closely by academic issues and behavioral concerns. For males, career and academic problems are equally important, followed by behavioral management.

COUNSELING OUTCOMES

Although some work has been done on overall counseling outcomes (Meltzoff and Kornreich, 1970), there is little conclusive research on the differential outcomes for men and women. Moreover, most of the studies are concerned primarily with outcomes of psychotherapy. In the absence of any research specific to the outcomes of career counseling, we can examine findings from the psychotherapeutic literature in order to infer sex differences in counseling outcome. Psychotherapy outcome studies investigating sex as a variable have reported no difference in outcomes, length of hospitalization or termination (Cartwright, 1955; Rosenthal and Frank, 1958; Lazarus, 1963; Esterson, Cooper, and Laing, 1965). Most research is of poor quality because of either the instruments or the experimental conditions. A few studies do report better results with females. M. C. Luff and M. Garrod (1935) report more frequent improvement in neurotic females than males, while C. R. Rogers and R. F. Dymond (1954) indicate greater improvement in females than in males in counselor judgments and adjustments. Studies with children indicated slightly better results with girls than boys (Rodriguez, Rodriguez and Eisenberg, 1959; Sobel, 1962; Warren, 1965; Hare, 1966). In contrast, some studies reported better results with males. J. H. Friedman (1950) indicated that males respond better to short-term therapy for travel phobia and S. Rachman (1965) and E. Schmidt, D. Castell, and P. Brown (1965) reported better results in behavior therapy with males.

In determining whether sex discrimination occurs in counseling, one must consider what constitutes an acceptable outcome. Many measurements of counseling outcome developed in traditional approaches to counseling are themselves biased. Traditional psychotherapy has been criticized for encouraging women to look inside themselves rather than at the surrounding society for the sources of their anxiety. A consequence of the traditional approach is that the outcomes are unclear, depending on whether it is the individual's or society's goals that are considered first in evaluating the functioning of a client. M. H. Klein (1975) argued that traditional mental health concepts stress adjustment to a role as opposed to the individual realizing his/her uniqueness.

According to Klein, there are five areas of disagreement between traditional and feminist views of counseling outcomes. The first concerns the definition of the presenting problem and, thereby, the determination of its outcome. The feminist view suggests that there is bias in the definition of life problems and the extent to which these are solved in counseling. This is especially the case when a women seeks treatment for problems that involve her whole family, but that she perceives as her own.

A second closely related outcome is that of quality of interpersonal relationships. One assumption of successful therapy is the improvement of these relationships. If counseling trains the woman to better meet the expectations of friends and family, however, this success may perpetuate the source of the problem that brought the woman to therapy in the first place. Thus this outcome, if used in the traditional way, can be a deceptive measure of successful therapy.

A third area is symptom removal. If the symptoms are seen as internal to the client, as in the traditional view, rather than societally induced, the responsibility for reduction is also internal rather than external. Since symptom removal is a basic criterion for the success of therapy, a biased determination of the source of the problem may result in an incorrect evaluation of the outcome of the therapy.

A fourth related area is role performance. The traditional view constricts possible role assignments by sex. Moreover, the evaluation of occupational ability and role performance is accomplished with biased instruments (see Chapter 5). A woman's helplessness and lack of motivation are not surprising, given these external constraints. Thus, to use successful role performance as a criterion for success of therapy would frequently be misleading.

Finally, the improvement of self-esteem is frequently a hoped-for outcome of therapy. Nonetheless, Klein notes that sexist stereotypes underlie many measures of self-esteem. An increase in measured self-esteem at the conclusion of therapy may in fact indicate acceptance of the conformity to stereotypes rather than positive change.

Klein's contrast between traditional counseling approaches and those with a feminist perspective highlights the changes needed to eliminate sex bias. Traditional theory provides outcome measures that focus primarily on "identifying or describing the values and cultural demands, and assessing adjustment in terms of stable, shared behavior patterns or personality traits" (p. 14).

SUMMARY AND IMPLICATIONS FOR GUIDANCE AND COUNSELING

Most conclusions about the impact of counseling are based on students' perceptions of their counseling experiences, supplemented by some counselors' studies of the impact of their services.

Although only about one-fifth of high school students of both sexes seek out counselors, females are slightly more likely than males to do so. Of all ethnic groups, blacks are somewhat more likely to confer with a guidance counselor over future plans, although the numbers are relatively small.

Most high school students (over 80 percent) of both sexes and all races think that they can see a counselor when they need to. About 80 percent think guidance counselors usually have the information they need. Only 60 percent are satisfied with the overall excellence of the guidance and counseling.

College women initiate counseling earlier in the academic year than men. Chinese-American females are the highest users of mental health services (Sue and Kirk, 1974). Only 17 percent of Mexican-American students use counseling services (Perez, 1975). Mexican-American students are less positive about therapy and counseling and have less confidence in mental health workers than nonminority group students.

There is no clear relationship between the sex of the client and counseling. Alternative formulations are needed for counseling outcomes and goals for women, since traditional outcome concepts are heavily sex biased.

There is no systematic treatment of counseling outcomes for women. Although much more research is needed, care must be exercised because traditional measurements are encrusted with sex bias.

More research is needed to determine which kinds of counselors affect clients in what ways. Data indicate that counselors do not influence high school students much. What are they doing that contributes to this lack of impact? Is the sparsity of counselors and their overload responsible?

A national study of interaction between counselors and students should be conducted to learn what counselors are telling students and what messages students are getting. Counseling centers must keep records of clients by sex and race. Finally, students on college campuses must be made aware of the various available counseling services.

CHAPTER

7

ALTERNATIVES
TO TRADITIONAL
COUNSELING

Although the picture of sex discrimination in guidance and counseling at the secondary and postsecondary level is bleak, the view is not without relief. Beginning with the feminist movement and spurred on by the Women's Educational Equity Act and public debate on equal rights, activities aimed at combating sexism in educational institutions and at expanding opportunies for girls and women have surged forward. Individual counselors and researchers, parent-community organizations, school boards, professional associations, the federal government, and others have set up task forces, developed guidelines, invented or revised techniques, and established programs to ensure equality of treatment and opportunities for men and women.

SEX-FAIR COUNSELING

It is impossible to evaluate the impact of potential sex discrimination in counseling without considering a number of antecedents. Beyond human factors, institutional structure and policies, as well as curricular and extracurricular activities and materials, may contribute to sex bias in guidance and counseling services. In examining alternatives for equal treatment of and opportunities for both sexes, it is not sufficient to review only those interventions that take place at the high school and post-high school level. Since sex-role stereotypes and socialization experiences that arbitrarily restrict the options of both sexes begin early, it is imperative to examine and propose strategies to eliminate sex discrimination throughout students' educational experience.

Task Forces on Sexism in the Schools

The impact of discriminatory treatment of boys and girls on their future alternatives and achievements is not unrecognized. The establishment of task forces within individual schools, school districts, and state departments of education is widespread (Committee to Eliminate Sex Discrimination, 1972; Ahlum, 1974; State of North Carolina, n.d.). These task forces generally have the same goal: To identify sex discrimination and to propose guidelines and strategies for its elimination. In each case a committee or task force identifies sexism within educational policies and practices and develops guidelines and strategies for its removal. The guidelines emphasize the importance of the student as an individual who should receive equitable treatment in and access to all areas of school life, regardless of sex. Increasing the entire educational community's awareness of the pervasive influence of sex-role stereotypes is a prerequisite for change. Committees identify and recommend nonsexist alternatives in guidance and counseling, curriculum, instructional materials, facilities, physical education, and interscholastic activities that affect a student's development and future opportunities. Guidance objectives include the following:

1. to encourage students of all ages to develop their own interests and talents as individuals rather than as members of a sex group.
2. to encourage all students to take part in life planning as individuals and as family members.
3. to encourage girls to take their talents seriously and explore traditionally male classes and fields, and to warn boys of the hazards of the "superman" role.
4. to make both sexes at all age levels aware of all occupations. Girls need to understand the value of a job or career for self sufficiency and self-fulfillment (State of North Carolina, n.d.).

Guidance-Related Professional Associations

A number of professional guidance associations have formed commissions to deal with sex bias in their ranks. In March 1972, the American Personnel and Guidance Association (APGA), acknowledging the "clear and undeniable evidence that girls and women suffer from personal and institution discrimination" and that the concern of counseling and guidance is "for the welfare of all human beings," established a Commission for Women (APGA, 1974, p. 1). The commission is responsible for investigating and reporting the status of women in the APGA, formulating recommendations, and guiding affirmative action programs within APGA, its divisions and branches. The Haun study (Haun, 1974; see Chapter 4), which examined sex distribution of counselor educators by faculty rank, was an outcome of the formation of the APGA Commission for Women. Similarly, the B. O. Pressley survey of guidance and counseling divisions of state departments of education was a product of the commission (Pressley, 1974). Other groups include the Association for Measurement and Evaluation in Guidance (AMEG), which, at the request of the APGA senate, developed a guide to evaluate sex bias in interest inventories. Another group is the Task Force on Sex Bias and Sex Role Stereotyping, established in 1975 by the American Psychological Association (APA), which focuses on the effect of psychotherapeutic practices on women as students, practitioners, and consumers.

A survey conducted by the task force of 2,000 women in APA identified four major areas of sex bias or sex-role stereotyping in psychotherapy that are equally applicable to counseling: (1) fostering traditional sex roles; (2) bias in expectations and devaluation of women; (3) sexist use of psychoanalytic concepts; and (4) responding to female clients as sex objects, including seduction. The most pressing need is "for consciousness raising, increased sensitivity, and greater awareness of the problems of sex bias and sex-role stereotyping in psychotherapeutic practices" (APA Task Force, 1975, p. 1174).

COUNSELING INTERVENTIONS

Can counseling practices evolve programs that give full consideration to an individual's feelings and help generate a range of alternatives irrespective of the client's sex or the counselor's value system? Recognizing sex discrimination and outlining potential remedies are only a start toward a solution. Nonsexist materials and techniques are needed to implement any plan to eradicate sex bias and sex-role stereotyping. N. K. Schlossberg (1974) suggested that "liberated" or nonsexist counseling requires good helping skills and sex-role consciousness raising by counselor and client.

Nonsexist Curricula and Counseling Programs

Sex-role consciousness raising is the focus of many program alternatives. Counselors may promote sex-role awareness within the school by many vehicles. Day-to-day curriculum has an impact on students' development, educational and vocational aspirations, and self-image. It is one mode by which sex-role consciousness raising can be presented. A number of nonsexist curriculum guides are available to assist counselors and teachers in their consciousness-raising efforts. One guide, *Today's Changing Roles: An Approach to Non-Sexist Teaching* (Resource Center on Sex Roles, 1974), presents supplementary instructional materials to help students explore and understand how sex-role stereotypes define and limit male and female roles. The purpose of these materials is to make students aware of sex-role stereotypes; to explore the implications of societal expectations for males and females; to analyze stereotypes, their sources, purposes, and the expectations and limitations they inflict on the individual; and to examine the ways in which stereotypes affect students' lives and futures.

L. S. Hansen (1972) presented a variety of extracurricular programs that counselors can implement to reduce sex-role stereotyping and promote equal development of both sexes' vocational and lifestyle plans. Because of the limited role models presented to girls, group counseling for girls to explore a variety of life patterns and the ramifications of each particular role is recommended. Hansen suggested that this exploration include the differences between facts and myths of women and work and women's contributions to society. "Strength groups," in which boys and girls focus on their potential and develop action plans for becoming the kinds of persons they would like to be, also facilitate individual development. Value clarification is an important related process for high school students. Students, as they begin to make vocational decisions, should be aware of discrimination in hiring, promotion, and salaries. Work experience is also valuable to students for reality testing. Students should also recognize the subtle ways in which society imposes its values, restricting the individual's free choice of life options.

Career counseling models that seek to build young women's awareness of myths and facts about women and work include Birk and Tanney's (1972) model. This model seeks to heighten women's awareness of the influence of sexism and stereotypic attitudes on their roles and career goals and proposes to broaden students' concept of what women's roles could be. Designed for junior and senior high school students, the model involves three one-hour group sessions and an informal individual follow-up with a counselor. An assessment of the model at one large high school yielded favorable increases in students' awareness of women's roles, career options, and the importance of life planning. I. M. Tiedt (1972) proposed a "realistic counseling model for high school girls." She stressed that most high school girls, especially those of lower socioeconomic background, are unaware of the high probability of their future need for employment. The model presents ten suggestions for counseling activities to provide girls with a more realistic picture of their own uncertain future and of the actual labor market situation for women.

Such career counseling programs need to be bolstered both by nonsexist career materials and by counselors who actively encourage nontraditional options for both sexes. Over 100 careers for women, many of them nontraditional, were explored by J. S. Mitchell (1975). For each career option, Mitchell presented a description of the field by a woman working in it. Educational requirements, the number and location of women in the field, beginning salaries, future opportunities, colleges awarding the most degrees to women in that field, and sources of further information are provided. The emphasis of this career counseling resource book is on choosing a satisfactory job, not simply a "female" job, but one that fits individual interests and talents and optimizes potential. This freedom of choice is available to women if they free themselves from their own stereotypic attitudes and develop a life style congruent with their own career development.

ABT Associates in Cambridge, Massachusetts has developed nonsexist career guidance kits, games, and resource guides. Other resources are identified in the *New Woman's Survival Sourcebook* (Rennie and Grimstad, 1975).

In-Service Counselor Training

The challenge of providing nonsexist counseling confronts counselors and counselor trainers whose formal training is highly traditional. Sex bias in the theories underlying much counseling practice, Freudian postulates, personality theory, and vocational development theory have been explored and found to be male oriented. They discriminate either by ignoring women or women's issues in theoretical treatises, by limiting women's options to traditionally feminine career or life patterns, and by labeling more "instrumental" or masculine preferences as deviant for women (Weisstein, 1971; Doherty, 1973; Mitchell, 1974; Laws, 1975). Traditional counselor training tends to rely on sex-biased theories, textbooks, and tools. Usually, no courses specifically about girls and women are provided. Recognition of this deficiency in traditional counselor training programs has spawned a number of programs, workshops, and handbooks aimed at helping counselors-in-training and in the field recognize and reduce sex bias. Some of these are described below.

The Sex Equality and Guidance Opportunities (SEGO) program, funded by the U.S. Office of Education and managed by APGA, has trained interested and qualified individuals from each state to conduct workshops for counselors and educators in their own state. The objectives are: (1) to expand awareness of instances of sex discrimination and bias in the environment and its illegality under Title IX of the Educational Amendments of 1972; (2) to examine the double discrimination against minority girls; (3) to expand options available to boys and girls by supplying information, resources, and techniques, and (4) to expand the influence of each workshop by having each participant develop a strategy for change within his/her own environment.

A "Workshop on New Careers" for postsecondary school and agency counselors (conducted in June 1974) was cosponsored by the APGA, the American Council on Education, the National Institute of Education, and the University of Maryland. The workshop was designed to (1) stimulate counselors to develop greater awareness of sex-role stereotypes, (2) provide career development and counseling skills, and (3) encourage participants to develop meaningful programs in their own settings. Speakers focused on the sociocultural sex-role norms that influence human beings in their vocational choices and behaviors and specific techniques that can help both sexes free themselves of sex-role stereotypes so that they may reach their full potential.

In-service training is also provided in conferences such as that conducted by the University of California, Los Angeles, Extension in 1973. The goal of the conference was to provide professionals with directions for acquiring the knowledge, techniques, and awareness to develop effective programs for women. A community-based effort to improve career counseling and programming for women, the conference emphasized skills development. Methods to assess women's needs in the context of social, economic, political, and educational trends were presented. The establishment of goals within institutional objectives and the development of guidelines for the content of women's programs were outlined. The development of counseling and teaching skills for working with women were reviewed, as was an assessment of the effectiveness of women's programs.

Two national associations, the American Association of University Women (AAUW) and the National Vocational Guidance Association (NVGA), have published books to aid teachers, counselors, and professionals concerned with maximizing human potential. *Liberating Our Children, Ourselves* (Howard, 1975) is a guide for developing women's studies course materials. The guide recommends that a women's studies program include courses or sections that examine sex differences and socialization and encourage each teacher and student to explore his/her sex biases. Counselors and teachers-in-training should also develop tools, methodologies, and materials that identify and eliminate sex-role stereotyping in school policies, programs, and materials. This resource book presents a comprehensive course syllabus with an outline, detailed objectives, learning projects, and an extensive bibliography for a women's studies program to be incorporated into a counselor or teacher education program or into a high school or college curriculum. *Counseling Girls and Women Over the Life Span* (Whitfield and Gustav, 1972) was developed by NVGA to increase the awareness by counselors, counselor trainers, and other professionals of the unique assets and needs girls and women bring to life situations. The life stages of women, the development of sex differences, and the social context within which women function are presented and the implications for counseling discussed. Special topics, such as value clarification for women, socialization, institutional barriers to women, and counseling in the year 2000 are also covered.

COUNSELING ALTERNATIVES FOR WOMEN

Efforts to meet the unique needs women bring to life situations have resulted in the development and modification of counseling alternatives for women. Three alternatives that illustrate the types of concerns are assertion training, feminist counseling, and continuing education for women.

Assertion Training

Assertiveness is the direct, honest, and appropriate expression of one's thoughts, opinions, feelings, or needs. Assertive behavior involves a high regard for one's own personal rights and the rights of others. Assertion training as a behavior intervention is increasingly offered in groups for women only. Women who are trying to function in roles outside the home often find themselves relating to others with types of behavior that interfere with their effectiveness as leaders and decision makers, problem solvers, or simply persons with their own ideas and self-interests to promote or personal rights to protect.

Assertion training involves helping the client to identify specific types of behavior that are unsatisfying and to specify their dysfunctional consequences. Then the belief system and self-statements that led a woman to choose this particular dysfunctional behavior are made explicit. The next step is to identify the client's preferred behavior, making explicit the belief system and self-statements that would lead to this choice and to maintaining it as a behavioral change. The client may have difficulty making the change, because the preferred behaviors are not presently within her repertoire or because the supportive belief system and statements to self may be absent. When assertion training is done in a group setting, the group plays a crucial role in supporting and encouraging behavioral change, as well as supplying feedback on the accuracy and appropriateness of the client's attempts at assertive behavior during role-play exercises and behavioral rehearsals.

The sex-role stereotyping of behavior presents women with special problems in the actual performance of assertive behavior. Women often find themselves making statements to others that are assertive in content but unassertive or aggressive in delivery and attendant body language. This may result either from the woman's real ambivalence about being assertive or from the absence in her behavioral repertoire of body language and speaking behavior that should appropriately accompany assertive statements. Among the various techniques for behavioral change employed in assertion training, video feedback is especially useful (Whiteley, 1973, 1975).

Feminist Counseling

Many feminist psychologists, counselors, and psychiatrists are creating independent theoretical perspectives on the psychology of women. The development of a feminist counseling approach involves three major thrusts: constructing a developmental psychology of women, identifying and analyzing the negative consequences for women of their socialization, and providing alternative formulations of presenting problems and counseling goals for women clients.

New ways to conceptualize the self-actualized woman and to identify developmental stages that reflect the realities of contemporary woman's greater control over her body and reproduction are being suggested by feminist psychologists. Previously ignored growth areas such as autonomy, identity, body image, sources of self-esteem, sexuality, and career development are also being studied and concepts of man-woman relationships are being formulated. Attempts are being made to integrate these into a comprehensive developmental framework (Klein, 1975; Westervelt, 1973).

Another major thrust of feminist psychology is an examination of the negative consequences of sex-role socialization (Wyckoff, 1974a, 1974b; Weisstein, 1971). R. Whiteley (1973) described the negative socialization of women:

> The culture conspires against woman at all stages of her life and denies her personal power. The denial pervades the legal structure, the economic structure, her religious life, family life, and probably most destructive of all, the psyche of the woman herself. From the moment of birth the culture carefully feeds back to her its view of her nature, its expectations which she must adopt for herself, and systematically rewards passive, deferential, dependent behavior (p. 33).

To remedy the effects of this negative socialization, intervention strategies must be developed and applied to help women overcome the handicaps and limitations imposed on their development. Some intervention strategies, such as assertion training and sex counseling, focus on individual behavior change. Others involve personal growth experiences of cognitive nature, for example, consciousness-raising groups, women's communal experiences, and exposure to women's arts and history. Still others involve developing competence in traditionally "masculine" areas and emphasizing career development for self-sufficiency and self-fulfillment.

Another change involves a different formulation of presentation of problems in therapy and of outcome goals for women clients. Contemporary women are experiencing psychological problems different from those they faced in the past; they need skills and support to handle problems with important environmental resources. E. M. Westervelt (1973) noted that "today's woman has been socialized to live in a world that no longer exists, . . . to acquire behavior styles that ill fit the responsibilities she is likely to carry" (p. 22). This discrepancy is the basis of many problems women bring to counseling: (1) integration of career, marriage, and family plans; (2) change in self-concept and in sources of self-esteem; (3) confusion in late adolescence over choices among life styles and gender roles because of intense pressure for sexual and emotional intimacy with men; and (4) the conflict of the older woman "[who] embarks upon a search for identity at a time in life when, . . . most of her male peers and some of her female peers have long since surmounted this developmental hurdle" (pp. 21-24).

Traditional counseling outcome goals do not take into account societal changes. M. H. Klein (1975) sets the major focus in counseling women as distinguishing between problems that are societally caused and those that are character disorders. She reported on feminist goals for counseling women:

"What is the connection between her pain, symptoms, and life situation? Is she reacting to role conflict or frustrating unsatisfying goals?

"Is her self-esteem dependent on others' evaluation and reactions or based on her own judgment and values?"

"Are her ideals and role choices influenced by traditional sexist stereotypes?" (pp. 15-16)

In addition to providing a framework of a feminist intervention system, the questions Klein presented may serve to encourage revision of traditional counseling theories.

Continuing Education Programs for Women

Often adult women, after examining their current situation and future opportunities, want and need to return to postsecondary institutions for further education or training. Because higher education has been structured for the "typical" student who completes his/her education through continuous, full-time study, adult women frequently experience institutional, as well as personal, barriers. Obstacles facing women who reenter the higher educational system include lack of information about resuming education and preparing for and beginning a career, lack of self-confidence, and time and financial constraints. These women may also have to deal with guilt feelings about abandoning their traditional home roles and actively seeking the education they want.

Continuing education programs for women (CEW) were developed to help women make the transition from home to college or work with a minimum of extraneous complications. Counseling is common to almost all CEW programs. Through individual or group counseling, women learn to assess themselves more realistically in an atmosphere supportive of self-exploration. The emphasis is usually on becoming aware of one's strong points, that is, capabilities, values, and aptitudes. Testing is often part of this self-evaluation process. Information about existing programs and vocational information are both available. If a woman wants to become a legal assistant, the counseling service can tell her about—or show her how to find—programs that offer this specialty.

In group counseling, women who have returned to work, combining career and family, are often invited to share their experiences and feelings. Employers speak on humanpower needs and job opportunities and requirements. Representatives from the college or university discuss academic requirements, courses, the demand for graduates, and the academic success of mature students. Often skills such as how to write a job resume or handle a job interview are taught. Support from counselors or other women in the group is an essential aspect of the counseling situation for most women, providing the reassurance and social approval they need to act. Through the counseling experience and self-analysis, women learn more about themselves and the realities of the current academic and work worlds. Armed with this information, they are in a much stronger position to make and implement decisions.

Each continuing education program differs from the others, but the common goal is to facilitate the back-to-school transition. The programs serve as intermediaries with the parent institutions, helping women handle rigid academic regulations or bypass them through admittance to the institution via continuing education. Counseling helps each woman in her search for direction and supplies her with information about options (H. S. Astin, 1976).

SUMMARY AND IMPLICATIONS FOR GUIDANCE AND COUNSELING

Many novel programs and counseling approaches can be utilized in more traditional settings.

Task forces in the schools are identifying sexism within educational policies and practices and developing guidelines and strategies for its removal. All guidelines emphasize the importance of the student as an individual who should receive equitable treatment in and access to all areas of school life, regardless of sex.

Guidance objectives have been set up for counselors by school board committees. Several professional societies have also set up commissions on women.

Sex-role consciousness raising is the focus of many alternative counseling programs. Several career counseling models have been developed to build young women's awareness of myths and facts about women and work, a first step toward more realistic life planning. The emphasis is on choosing a satisfactory job, not simply a female job, but one that fits the individual's interests and talents and optimizes her potential.

Several workshops have been set up for counselors from elementary school through college. Handbooks and guides have been developed to aid teachers, counselors, and all professionals in maximizing human potential.

Traditional counseling theories and practices reflect the sex-role stereotyping and sexual bias prevalent in society. Counselors interested in optimizing the potential of all individuals, regardless of sex, must seek out and implement new theories and practices that provide individuals with the broadest range of alternatives. Individual counselors, professional associations, feminist organizations, and private publishers are producing nonsexist resources for counseling. Several factors, however, work against their effectiveness. Traditional and sexist materials continue to be produced by well-known publishing houses and to compete with nonsexist materials. Persuading school boards to approve and counselors to use innovative approaches and materials poses problems of reeducation and consciousness raising. While nonsexist revisions of counseling techniques and programs are available, their reliability and validity are yet to be tested. While much remains to be done, it is imperative that counselors-in-training and those in the field be exposed to nonsexist techniques and materials and begin to test and incorporate them into school counseling and curriculums.

Counselor education and reeducation may be major tools in ridding schools of sexism. While each program, workshop, and guide includes rich and varied materials to help counselors develop nonsexist counseling and curriculums, their effectiveness is limited. Most traditional counselor education programs do not include courses on women's issues, though there is some evidence that this weakness is being remedied. The responsibility rests with counselors in the field to avail themselves of in-service programs to develop greater sensitivity to the issues of sex bias and stereotyping. These professionals can then be catalysts within their environment to raise others' consciousness to ensure equal opportunity for men and women.

CHAPTER

8

IMPLICATIONS
AND RECOMMENDATIONS

The purpose of guidance and counseling is to facilitate students' life adjustment, role clarification, and self-understanding. Evaluation of the sex fairness or sex bias in guidance and counseling at the secondary level and beyond is complicated by the socialization process. Students, counselors, teachers, and parents all learn sex-appropriate behaviors, attitudes, and aspirations and internalize cultural sex stereotypes. The institutions within which they function are products of these cultural conditions.

Analysis of overt sex discrimination in counselor attitudes and counseling materials is insufficient to determine the dimension of sex bias confronting both boys and girls in high school and later. Knowledge of the sex stereotypes that children have internalized through earlier socialization and of what other agents of socialization—parents, teachers, books, movies, television, peers—are currently teaching students about their appropriate sex roles is essential to evaluate the success of counseling and guidance in optimizing an individual's alternatives regardless of sex.

SOCIALIZATION

Recommendations, based on the findings of Chapter 2, are many:

First, elementary schools could profit from some curricular interventions. Because the effects of discrimination are cumulative and elementary school is a key time for programmatic work, career development interventions should be made at this early stage. The need to understand the impact of this programmatic thrust warrants an evaluation component in each programmatic effort. Moreover, special guidance material and curriculums should be available at the elementary school level. New materials should be developed and existing in-class materials, such as readers and other textbooks, revised.

115

Other interventions are based on needed research. For example, researchers need to determine how to resocialize the sexes: Specifically, what kinds of activities, interactions, and materials would be effective?

Research findings indicate that during adolescence women regress in educational and social development. This regression coincides with biological and hormonal change. A research question that has not been answered is: What happens to young girls at that time in terms of preparing for motherhood and career? Interventions with young men, as well as young women, are needed for sex-role restructuring, because they are the future mates, bosses, colleagues, and subordinates of young women.

Other research questions that must be answered are: Do existing theoretical works on achievement motivation provide an adequate explanation for women's achievement behavior? To what extent do other variables, such as self-concept and sex-role attitudes, affect women's achievement? Does attribution theory provide a valid, alternative explanation for differential achievement? What are the forces in the development of minority students that contribute to lower self-esteem and achievement motivation? Do such patterns warrant change?

In training personnel, teachers must give special attention to nontraditional careers for women. This recommendation implies additions to the teacher education curriculum, consciousness raising, and revision of the attitudes of teachers so they do not treat the sexes differently. This recommendation applies to teachers at all levels. Administrators must also be sensitized to allow certain novel materials into the schools. Counselors must be made aware of socialization and sex-role research. They must be taught techniques based on the research on sex-role socialization to counteract harmful socialization. Counselors must also be made aware of their own biases.

Moreover, inadequate information and poor research on minority socialization results in misunderstandings by the majority population, including teachers, researchers, counselors, and administrators. More and higher-quality research and consciousness raising on minority issues must be undertaken for these groups.

Changing the attitudes of current school personnel alone cannot have a great impact. More nontraditional role models must be provided. For example, male elementary teachers should be recruited in greater numbers and visits by police officers or fire fighters should include representatives of both sexes.

Similarly, training must be undertaken with the students themselves. For example, both boys and girls must be trained not only in career awareness, but also in what it means to be a family member. Alternatives must be generated for the usually rigid sex roles. Boys and girls must be encouraged to communicate with one another about their perception of sex roles.

Changes in acceptable ways for self-actualization should be introduced. Society must accept values that allow a young man who does not want a career to actualize himself in other ways. Counselors must be actively involved in raising the consciousness of both men and women and facilitating their understanding and acceptance of themselves and one another.

Helpful interventions should change students' locus of control and perception of power. Value clarification exercises could change values on an individual basis rather than on a male/female continuum. Counselors are responsible for enlarging the options.

SOCIALIZATION AND TRAINING OF COUNSELORS

The recommendations in this area are of three kinds: those having to do with composition of the counseling profession, with preparation of counselors, and with research.

First, more female counselor educators need to be hired. Since many more women earn doctorates in areas appropriate for counselor educators than are hired for such positions, the unavailability of qualified women is not an issue; rather, affirmative action must be practiced.

Similarly, more female students should be recruited for graduate programs in counseling. To enroll a more representative group of counseling students, students of both sexes and of minority status should be exposed while in high school to counseling as a job possibility.

In addition, faculty rank should be equalized, since more men now hold high level faculty positions than women. Women are hired at the assistant professor level and often not given tenure. The implication (aside from the obvious inequity) is that students see powerful male department heads and weak female assistant professors and may conclude that women will never rise beyond a certain level. This situation discourages female students from aspiring to higher educational and career levels, since they do not have appropriate role models.

Materials used in training counselors need to be systematically reviewed for bias. For example, textbooks used in graduate training should be carefully reviewed, and guidelines provided to or by the publisher. Neuter expressions or the use of both masculine and femine nouns and pronouns should be adopted as standard publishing procedure. The American Psychological Association's (APA) recent addition to the publication guidelines is a good model. Similarly, materials for those now being trained in counseling must be developed, as well as for those who have already been trained. A book on guidance and counseling that brings together female psychology and counseling should be written.

Those already trained should be required as part of their certification to take in-service training on nonsexist counseling. In conjunction, contracts awarded to develop and package in-service training materials must be brought to the attention of educators.

Courses on counseling girls and women must be added to the counselor training curriculum. The likelihood that such courses would be well received is high, since most departments surveyed by Pressley (1974) indicated a desire for this type of course. Courses on minority students should also be encouraged. Supervision and field experience with both groups should be required of the training program. All these recommendations should be requirements for counselor certification. Whether successful teaching should be given major weight in counselor certification is unclear. Instead, field experience and course work should be increased.

Finally, counseling and vocational development theories must be examined carefully by counselor trainees. Ways in which existing theories are dysfunctional to women's development should be discussed.

In research, information is needed on the role of minorities in the counseling field, especially nonblack minorities. In particular, the total lack of research on American Indians is salient.

Additional research should study the recipients of services and the system. State departments should set standards for training which would include anti-bias regulations. Similarly, professional associations should be encouraged to adopt guidelines for training programs to eliminate sex bias. The APA, for example, could withhold approval from programs of school and counseling psychology if they did not meet the guidelines. Moreover, the American Personnel and Guidance Association and other professional guidance associations could publish statements encouraging nonsexist training.

COUNSELING PROCESS

Recommendations on the counseling process concern counselor behaviors and attitudes and counseling materials (tests, handbooks, and so forth).

The effects of the race and sex of the counselor on counseling outcomes are ambiguous, although the sex of the counselor may be related to certain kinds of counselor behavior. Counselors, however, generally have stereotypic attitudes toward women who behave in nontraditional ways. Many women who do not conform to the norm—whether by choosing careers in engineering, by not marrying, or by displaying traditionally masculine qualities such as assertiveness—meet with resistance from counselors.

To correct these biases, counselor educators should concentrate on raising counselors' consciousness of race and sex stereotypes. At the same time, schools that employ counselors should provide consciousness-raising sessions specifically to combat sex-stereotypic attitudes, and counselors should examine their individual attitudes toward women.

Finally, more information on careers, financial aid, colleges, apprenticeships, and jobs should be provided to counselors, since many operate under incorrect assumptions.

Several groups are already refining tests and career guidance materials. This kind of change, however, is slow to come, and it is likely that tests and materials will not change much in the near future. Therefore, both institutions and individuals have a responsibility when they use these materials. Counselors should use new nonsexist materials when available. Until those are readily available, counselors must raise questions about every tool they use, whether it is an interest inventory, a career brochure, college catalog, or the *Occupational Outlook Handbook*. They must ask whether the information or the text reflect stereotypic roles for men and women, and whether the materials tend to close certain career options for either sex. Then they must counteract the stereotypic assumptions. The counselor and the client have an opportunity to confront and explore sex-role biases as they emerge in the counseling session and to pursue avenues that are broadening rather than binding.

Institutions should rewrite their catalogs to reflect nonsexist intent. Government publications with vocational impact must also be rewritten. Colleges should provide special services for women students.

RESULTS OF COUNSELING

Studies on the results of counseling are lacking, of poor quality, or inconclusive, especially as they relate to sex bias. Programmatic research is needed on counseling outcomes. Specifically, what are the effects on the female student of seeing a counselor? Care must be exercised, however, because traditional measurements of counseling outcomes are encrusted with sex bias.

More research is needed to determine how particular characteristics of counselors affect clients.

All counseling centers must keep records of clients by sex and race (as an increasing number now do). Research should be undertaken to determine why counselors have so little influence on high school students. What causes this lack of impact? Is the sparsity of counselors and their overload responsible? At the college level, students must be made aware of all available counseling services. A national study of interaction between counselors and students is needed to ascertain what counselors are telling students and what messages students are getting.

Finally, it may be advisable to restructure the role of the school counselor so that he/she will have an opportunity to make an impact.

ALTERNATIVES TO TRADITIONAL COUNSELING

While there is progress in developing alternatives to traditional counseling, continued development of alternative programs, techniques, and materials must be encouraged.

Innovative materials must be approved by school boards and used by teachers. Development of materials alone, however, will not be sufficient.

Counselors should be exposed to nonsexist counseling techniques and testing, incorporating them into school counseling and curriculums. New approaches must also be brought into training programs, into reeducation sessions for counselors already certified, and into consciousness raising.

Finally, since women as a group vary, counselors and teachers must adopt a more multidimensional view toward them. Within the group of minority women, for instance, are blacks, Hispanics, Asians, and American Indians, and each group has subgroups (for example, among Hispanics are Cuban Americans, Puerto Ricans, and Mexican Americans). To consider that all women will get married is also erroneous. Some will be single parents, others will be married but the major contributor to the family, while still others may never marry. All these differences must be considered when dealing with women students.

SEX DISCRIMINATION IN EDUCATION

The findings presented in Chapter 3 have a number of implications that provide a framework for recommendations on programmatic efforts to be undertaken by postsecondary educational institutions. In addition, they suggest the need for research that can provide more and better information and for data collection methods.

It is evident that, if women are to have the same occupational opportunities as men do, steps must be taken by the secondary schools to ensure that they have the necessary preparation. First, high school girls who take vocational curriculums should be encouraged to diversify their fields of study from the typically "female" courses into the technical courses that are now the domain of boys. Second, high school girls enrolled in academic and college preparatory curriculums should be counseled to enroll in and complete more courses in mathematics and science. As the situation stands now, women often underprepare themselves in these areas because they fail to realize that such preparation considerably enlarges their options and thus may be crucial to their future lives.

Many young women continue to believe that postsecondary education bears little relation to their future lives—one reason why fewer women than men pursue postsecondary education. In addition, high school girls are more likely than high school boys to perceive the costs of a postsecondary education as a barrier. A lack of information about financial aid resources and a tendency to underprepare in science and mathematics both impede young women in formulating and implementing their postsecondary plans. Thus, in dealing with high school girls, counselors have a dual responsibility: To help them develop more realistic outlooks about their future lives, and to provide practical and detailed information about the financial costs of an education and about sources of financial aid.

Programmatic guidance efforts can assist all high school girls to (1) change their perceptions about appropriate occupational roles for women and (2) develop a better understanding of the multiple roles they are likely to assume in the future. Specific efforts in assisting women to prepare for the future might include specially designed courses on career development, to be taken by both girls and boys. Such courses would have two components: Self-assessment of interests and competencies, and occupational information, including what types of preparation are needed for different occupations, and what their requirements and rewards are. Such courses would emphasize—through discussions and analyses—how sex-role socialization shapes occupational choices and would seek to free students from these stereotypes.

Another step that should be taken at the curricular level is to introduce high school girls early to technical and scientific material so that their interest will be aroused and their sense of competency be developed.

We would recommend that women's studies be introduced in high school so that students of both sexes can gain a greater understanding of the effects of socialization. Women's studies can elucidate the images of woman as depicted in literature, history, and art as well as exposing the student to important women writers, artists, and scientists who may serve as role models.

The rather limited participation of women, and their concentration in traditionally female fields, results from socialization as to appropriate roles and occupations for women. Sex-role stereotypes continue to operate as women make decisions about their future lives. To overcome these stereotypes (which have already taken their toll in high school) colleges, and in particular technological institutions, should attempt to develop affirmative programs for women. Such programs would include special efforts to recruit high school girls to provide them with tutorials and remediation in mathematics and science once they have been admitted.

Colleges should continue to support women's studies, for the same reasons outlined earlier with respect to women's studies in high school. Moreover, since female role models are scarce in higher education in general—and in traditionally male fields in particular—special efforts are needed to give young women a chance to interact with role models, for instance, in workshops or seminars. Films on the lives and activities of successful women are a further example of possible programmatic efforts to provide role models for college women.

The lack of gynecological facilities and of day-care centers has been viewed as a form of sex discrimination in that many women need such support if they are to continue their education without undue pressure. To provide convenient and inexpensive health care, gynecological facilities should be made available as an integral part of any educational institution's medical services. One of the benefits is psychological: The provision of such facilities increases the woman's sense of belonging in the institution. Moreover, as long as a woman is expected by society to bear primary responsibility for her children and to follow her husband to a new location when he makes a change, an effort should be made to provide for child care and to permit part-time study. It would also help in such situations if institutions develop new and simpler ways of translating and accepting credit from other institutions, so that women who must follow their husbands do not lose credit for previous postsecondary experience.

Two substantive research needs emerge. The first is for periodic data collection from high school students in order to observe trends and changes in their plans and aspirations. Thus, we recommend that a program of research to collect data from high school students periodically and to follow up some of the cohorts be designed and instituted.

The second research need is for studies to identify the factors that influence the career decisions of women. We need to identify the personal characteristics, background, and early experiences of women who choose and pursue different fields and careers. Equally, we need to learn what variables stimulate or inhibit career development. Some of these studies may be cross-sectional, looking at young women of different ages, racial-ethnic backgrounds, and socioeconomic statuses with respect to their plans, choices, and preparation, or looking at women in different fields to identify their differentiating personal characteristics, early development experiences, and educational experiences. Other studies should be longitudinal, identifying the critical experiences in the lives of young women that result in differential aptitudes, interests, personal traits, and values—all presumably important determinants in career choice and development. For example, how do young children begin to form concepts about work and about themselves? What kinds of home environments and parent-child interactions develop autonomy, high self-esteem, and a sense of competence in a variety of areas? What educational experiences reinforce a sense of self-worth and competence? What role do a liberal arts program, a work-study experience, career guidance, or specialized mathematics curriculums play in developing aptitudes and competencies essential to appropriate career choice and development?

These studies should be framed in the context of educational institutions. The underlying question must always be: What institutional practices affect women's full development and utilization?

From this study of sex discrimination in educational access, other more specific research needs emerge.

1. To what extent do the limited career aspirations of women lead them to enter less selective and less affluent institutions? As we have seen, women aspire less frequently than men to technical and scientific careers, and this may lead them to choose smaller, more convenient, and less expensive colleges over universities where technical facilities are available. A study designed to test whether

women with different career aspirations select different types of institutions, independent of aptitudes or past achievements, would be useful in resolving this question.

2. The exploratory studies we undertook on admissions (described in the main report) suggest the need to explore further (a) the factors that influence women to apply to certain kinds of institutions and not others (this is an elaboration of the study described above), and (b) the rates of acceptance for women when aptitudes, high school preparation, and career interests are controlled.

3. Earlier, we recommend a number of curricular modifications and innovations. Such efforts should be accompanied by research to evaluate the changes that result from these curricular changes.

Finally, a word must be said about methods of data collection. Although surveys provide valuable information about some facets of educational and occupational development, they cannot assess more subtle and nonverbal areas. For example, teacher-student interactions, which may affect a woman's perception of herself, cannot be studied through surveys; interviews and observations are required.

Surveys are often limited in the way they ask for information from some populations. For example, asking a Chicano student whether her parents encouraged her to pursue higher education may be inappropriate in that other family members, such as an older brother, may play a more important role than the parents. Thus, a simple yes or no answer could be misleading. Interviews with these students, however, can highlight these nuances.

ADDITIONAL RESEARCH RECOMMENDATIONS

Recommendations for future research at the high school level include career development of minority women and men. More minority women than men complete high school and take postsecondary education. Disproportionate numbers of minority men may perceive that their options are limited to post-high school employment or to military service. The question is: How influential is the military in channeling minority men out of the educational mainstream?

Another research area is disadvantaged students. Traditionally, programs for the disadvantaged have tried to change individual students rather than the school system that produces those students. Of course, only students who are exposed to the programs are affected by them; disadvantaged students who are not enrolled do not benefit. Some educators suggest that the money spent on such programs could be better used to develop techniques to change the institutions that produce differentially prepared and motivated students. In similar fashion, women students may be considered disadvantaged in that they do not often have the opportunity, for instance, to enroll in industrial arts courses, and they are discouraged from hard sciences and mathematics. A great deal of money is spent to remedy these injustices ex post facto. Researchers should examine the school system and the counseling (both informal and formal) that result in differential treatment with an eye toward changing both.

Recommendations for research at the college level include examining the segmentation of college counseling services. Apparently, many colleges offer vocational services in one location, job counseling and placement services in another, financial aid counseling in a third, and personal-social counseling in still another. Does this specialization and lack of coordination have differential effects on men and women?

Also at the college level, there appears to be a hierarchy of responsiveness of the counselor to different student concerns. Many counselors give top status to personal-social counseling and second-class status to vocational counseling (Melnick, 1975; Hill et al., 1977). If individuals primarily interested in personal counseling end up counseling students on vocational goals, what effect will their attitudes have on the counseling a student receives?

While the impact of the sex or race of the student and counselor is still unclear, the way in which the counselor is assigned to the client may be an issue. Are the race and sex of both parties considered? Is a student assigned to the first counselor available?

Similarly, in counseling outreach programs, counselor sex may be an issue. In several colleges, counseling services are experimenting with outreach programs, where counselors are assigned to certain subject areas or to particular schools. Are men counselors assigned to engineering while women counselors work with home economics? Such assignments would have clear implications for the two sexes.

In vocational schools the focus of counseling is a little different. Since training is more oriented to the labor market, counseling also tends to focus on labor market issues. This raises several questions: Is counseling in vocational schools as stereotyped as the labor market? Are women students channeled into such careers as beautician, secretary, and dental hygienist while men are steered away from those fields? Is there any counseling for personal-social problems in vocational schools?

Since data are sparse, answering any of these questions is difficult. The only major study of vocational institutions (Wilms, 1974) does not focus on counseling. The 1974 Cooperative Institutional Research Program data on a preliminary segment of 19 schools make it possible to explore the percentage that will seek both types of counseling: About 4 percent of entering students project a need for both vocational and personal counseling. For colleges and universities, the figures are about 10 percent and 5 percent, respectively. College men and women project a need for both kinds of counseling in about equal numbers, but proprietary school men more often than women project a need for vocational counseling, while the reverse is true for personal counseling.

Finally, in vocational schools, it appears that the major emphasis on counseling comes at the beginning of school and at graduation. Any funneling of students into careers by sex probably occurs during the admissions process or the awarding of financial aid. Job placement counseling may be equally fair to both sexes, although no data support either supposition.

LEGISLATIVE RECOMMENDATIONS

This study was undertaken when Title IX of the Education Amendments of 1972 was enacted. The provisions in Title IX correspond closely to the findings of this study and to the recommendations.

Specifically, Title IX prohibits discrimination in counseling and in appraisal and counseling materials. The measure requires developers of counseling programs to use internal procedures to prevent such discrimination. Institutions themselves may have to determine whether a test or other criterion is biased and to look at the reasons for unbalanced results. Title IX also requires that catalogs and literature distributed by educational institutions reflect nondiscriminatory policy in both text and illustrations.

Not covered under Title IX are textbooks and curricular material protected under the free speech provisions of the First Amendment. Some states have attempted to get around this problem: California, for example, enacted Section 9240 of the California Education Code, which states:

> When adopting instructional materials for use in the schools, governing boards shall include only instructional materials which, in their determination, accurately portray the cultural and racial diversity of our society, including:
>
> a. The contributions of both men and women in all types of roles, including professional, vocational, and executive roles.
>
> b. The role and contributions of American Indians, American Negroes, Mexican Americans, Asian Americans, European Americans, and members of other ethnic and cultural groups to the total development of California and the United States.

Further, Section 8576, in a paragraph on instruction in the social sciences, states that:

> Instruction in social sciences shall include the early history of California and a study of the role and contributions of American

Negroes, American Indians, Mexicans, persons of Oriental extraction, and other ethnic groups, and the role and contributions of women, to the economic, political, and social development of California and the United States of America, with particular emphasis on portraying the roles of these groups in contemporary society.

Similar legislation should be enacted in every state. While Title IX addresses itself to the issues in this study, its enforcement it limited to administrative review by a small staff at the U.S. Department of Health, Education, and Welfare and does not provide for private right of action. Without private right of action, which allows an individual to sue an institution, Title IX can pose no real legal threat to institutions, especially since they have become sophisticated in avoidance tactics under Executive Order 12246. An amendment to provide for private right of action in a court of law is necessary.

APPENDIX
METHODS AND PROCEDURES

The three types of approaches used in this research are described below.

LITERATURE SEARCH

The literature reviewed has appeared primarily in the last decade except for "classic" studies. The method used to identify the documents included:

1. A cataloging and review of bibliographies, books, reprints (Astin, Parelman, and Fisher, 1975; Astin, Suniewick, and Dweck, 1974; Bickner, 1974; Harmon, 1972; Westervelt and Fixter, 1971; Phelps, Farmer and Backer, 1975; Padilla and Aranda, 1974).

2. Computer searches of the literature, including the APA (American Psychological Association) service, ERIC (Education Resource Information Center), CIJE (Current Index to Journals in Education) and RIE (Research in Education). Searches are made with key-word concepts.

DATA SOURCES

Data sources and statistical reports based on these sources include:

1. Project TALENT. In 1960, Project TALENT (sponsored by the Office of Education, U.S. Department of Health, Education, and Welfare) surveyed students in grades nine through twelve in a 5-percent stratified random sample of the nation's high schools. These students were followed up through mail questionnaires one, five, and eleven years after high school graduation. Special telephone follow-ups assured representativeness of the follow-up samples. At that time, TALENT collected background information on ability, SES, grades, curriculum, educational and career interests, and expectations, and follow-up data on educational, job, and personal experiences.

2. Cooperative Institutional Research Program (CIRP). The Cooperative Institutional Research Program, conducted jointly by the American Council on Education and the University of California at Los Angeles, began in 1966 with data collected from all entering freshmen at 307 representative institutions. Today, the sample includes over 600 institutions. The entire freshman class of participating institutions is surveyed upon matriculation. At subsequent intervals, subsamples of these same students are surveyed again.

The main purpose of the annual survey is to collect student data. The instrument is the Student Information Form (SIF), a four-page questionnaire designed to be self-administered under proctored conditions and to be processed onto magnetic tape by an optical scanner. Many of the approximately 200 SIF items, essentially the same from year to year, elicit standard biographical and demographic information from each student: for example, sex; racial/ethnic and religious background; parents' income, educational levels, and occupations; high school activities and achievements; means of financing college education; degree aspirations; probable major field; career plans; attitudes on social and campus issues; and life goals. Through repeated items, not only may successive cohorts of freshmen be compared to discover national trends in the chracteristics of entering students, but also the individual's responses on the SIF can be compared with his/her responses on follow-up questionnaires to see whether he/she has changed (for instance, in his/her political views or career plans) over time.

Items are added to the SIF as new areas of higher education become prominent. In 1971, when open admissions and programs for underprepared students were topics of special interest, freshmen were asked to indicate in which, if any, subjects they might need tutoring or remedial work. The SIF represents a compromise between two demands: the need for continuity to obtain comparable information and the need for flexibility to permit investigation of current issues.

3. National Scholarship Service and Fund for Negro Students (NSSFNS). The NSSFNS file provides information on a national sample of black high school seniors representing the high school classes of 1971–73. These data, collected as part of a program to provide counseling and guidance services to black youth, include demographic items, educational and occupational aspirations, attitudes, values, and high school experiences and achievements. For each year the data file includes information on about 50,000 black youth at approximately 7,000 high schools.

4. National Longitudinal Study of the High School Class of 1972. In spring 1972, over 1,000 high schools participated in a National Longitudinal Study of the high school class of 1972. Data were gathered from about 18,000 high school seniors. Follow-up data were collected a year after high school, and subsequent surveys are planned for a period of 6 to 8 years. Information includes student demographic characteristics, postsecondary plans, educational and occupational aspirations, and high school experiences and achievements.

EXPLORATORY STUDIES

Several exploratory studies were conducted to generate implications:

1. A list of 100 colleges and 19 proprietary institutions whose catalogs were analyzed was compiled. The colleges are representative of the CIRP institutions on selectivity, geographical location, control (public-private), and

type (two-year, four-year, predominantly black). Although the proprietary institutions included in the 1974 CIRP are not a statistical sample, they are representative of schools of different types and geographical locations.

2. The alumni offices of these same institutions sent results of any alumni surveys conducted in the last five years. Any data on satisfaction with college counseling experiences were abstracted.

3. One hundred programs of counselor education were randomly chosen from 400 programs cited in J. W. Hollis and R. A. Wantz (1974). Directors of these programs furnished information on their curriculums, including course readings and faculty, and self-studies or evaluations of their counseling centers.

4. A nationwide listing of requirements for counselor certification in the 50 states was analyzed for content.

5. Two exploratory studies in the Los Angeles high schools, one of the content of career and vocational guidance literature and the other of financial aid information, were conducted.

6. Counselor job descriptions in the Los Angeles schools were assessed for information on counselor workloads.

REFERENCES

Abramowitz, S. I., L. J. Weitz, J. M. Schwartz, S. Amira, B. Gomes, and C. V. Abramowitz. 1975. "Comparative Counselor Inferences toward Women with Medical School Aspirations." *Journal of College Student Personnel* 16 (2): 128–30.

Ahlum, C. 1974. "Kalamazoo: A Model for Change." *Inequality in Education*, no. 18: 47–52.

Almquist, E., and S. S. Angrist. 1971. "Role Model Influences on College Women's Career Aspirations." *Merrill-Palmer Quarterly* 17 (3): 263–79.

American College Testing Program (ACT). 1972a. *Counselors' Handbook, 1972–73*. Iowa City, Iowa: ACT.

——. 1972b. *Using ACT on Campus, 1972–73*. Iowa City, Iowa: ACT.

American Council on Education (ACE). 1975. "Federal Student Loan Programs." *Policy Analysis Service Reports* 1 (1). Washington, D.C.: ACE.

——. 1972. "The American Freshman: National Norms for Fall 1972." *ACE Research Reports* 7 (5). Washington, D.C.: ACE.

——. 1971. "The American Freshman: National Norms for Fall 1971." *ACE Research Reports* 6 (6). Washington, D.C.: ACE.

American Personnel and Guidance Association (APGA). 1974. *1973–74 Summary Report*. Washington, D.C.: APGA.

American Psychological Association (APA) Task Force. 1975. "Report on Sex Bias and Sex-role Stereotyping in Psychotherapeutic Practice." *American Psychologist* 30 (12): 1169–75.

Anastasi, A. 1968. *Psychological Testing*. New York: Macmillan.

Anderson, R. P., and G. Lawlis. 1972. "Strong Vocational Interest Blank and Culturally Handicapped Women." *Journal of Counseling Psychology* 19 (1): 83–84.

Association for Measurement and Evaluation in Guidance (AMEG). 1973. "AMEG Commission Report on Sex Bias in Interest Measurement." *Measurement and Evaluation in Guidance* 6 (3): 171–77.

Astin, A. W. 1975. *Preventing Students from Dropping Out*. San Francisco: Jossey-Bass.

——. 1970. "Racial Considerations in Admissions." In *The Campus and the Racial Crisis*, ed. D. C. Nichols and O. Mills, pp. 113–41. Washington, D.C.: ACE.

Astin, A. W., M. R. King, J. M. Light, and G. T. Richardson. 1974. *The American Freshman: National Norms for Fall 1974*. Los Angeles: ACE and the University of California.

Astin, A. W., R. J. Panos, and J. A. Creager. 1967. *National Norms for Entering College Freshmen–Fall 1966. ACE Research Reports* 2 (1).

Astin, H. S. 1975. "Young Women and Their Roles." In *Youth*, ed. R. J. Havighurst, part 1, pp. 419-34. Chicago: University of Chicago Press.

Astin, H. S., and A. E. Bayer. 1972. "Sex Discrimination in Academe." *The Educational Record* (spring): 101-18.

Astin, H. S., A. Parelman, and A. Fisher. 1975. *Sex Roles: A Research Bibliography*. Washington, D.C.: U.S. Government Printing Office.

Astin, H. S., N. Suniewick, and S. Dweck. 1974. *Women: A Bibliography on their Education and Careers*. New York: Behavioral Publications.

Astin, H. S. (ed.) 1976. *Some Action of Her Own: The Adult Woman and Higher Education*. Lexington, Mass.: D.C. Heath.

Attwood, C. L. 1972. *Women in Fellowship and Training Programs*. Washington, D.C.: Association of American Colleges, Project on the Status and Education of Women.

Backner, B. L. 1970. "Counseling Black Students: Any Place for Whitey?" *Journal of Higher Education* 41 (7): 630-37.

Baldwin, J. 1963. *The Fire Next Time*. New York: Dial Press.

Bandura, A., D. Ross, and S. A. Ross. 1961. "Transmission of Aggression through Imitation of Aggressive Models." *Journal of Abnormal and Social Psychology* 63 (3): 575-82.

Banks, G., B. Berenson, and E. Carkhuff. 1967. "The Effects of Counselor Race and Training upon Counseling Process with Negro Clients in Initial Interview." *Journal of Clinical Psychology* 23: 70-72.

Barron's Education Services, Inc. 1973. *Barron's Profile of American Colleges*, vol. 1, *Descriptions of the Colleges*. Woodbury, New York: Barron's.

Baruch, G. K. 1972. "Maternal Influences upon College Women's Attitudes toward Women and Work." *Developmental Psychology* 6 (1): 32-37.

Bayer, A. E. 1972. "The Black College Freshman: Characteristics and Recent Trends." *ACE Research Reports* 7 (3).

Bayer, A. E., and H. S. Astin. 1975. "Sex Differentials in the Academic Reward System." *Science* 188: 796-802.

Bayer, A. E., and R. F. Boruch. 1969. "The Black Student in American Colleges." *ACE Research Reports* 4 (2).

Bem, S. L., and D. J. Bem. 1973. "On Liberating the Female Student." *The School Psychology Digest* 2 (3): 10-18.

Bengelsdorf, W. 1974. *Women's Stake in Low Tuition*. Washington, D.C.: American Association of State Colleges and Universities.

Berger, C. R. 1968. "Sex Differences Related to Self-esteem Factor Structure." *Journal of Consulting and Clinical Psychology* 32 (4): 442-46.

Bernard, J. 1966. *Marriage and Family Among Negroes*. Englewood Cliffs, N.J.: Prentice-Hall.

Bernstein, J. 1972. "The Elementary School: Training Ground for Sex Role Stereotypes." *Personnel and Guidance Journal* 51 (2): 97-101.

Bickel, P. J., E. A. Hammel, and J. W. O'Connell. 1975. "Sex Bias in Graduate Admissions: Data from Berkeley." *Science* 187: 398-404.

Bickner, M. L. 1974. *Women at Work: An Annotated Bibliography*. Los Angeles: Institute of Industrial Relations, Manpower Research Center.

Billingsley, A. 1968. *Black Families in White America*. Englewood Cliffs, N.J.: Prentice-Hall.

Bing, E. 1963. "Effect of Childrearing Practices on Development of Differential Cognitive Abilities." *Child Development* 34: 631-48.

Bingham, W. C., and E. W. House. 1973a. "Counselors' Attitudes toward Women and Work." *Vocational Guidance Quarterly* 22: 16-23.

——. 1973b. "Counselors View Women and Work: Accuracy of Information." *Vocational Guidance Quarterly* 21 (4): 262-68.

Birk, J. M. 1975. "Reducing Sex-bias—Factors Affecting the Client's View of the Use of Career Interest Inventories." In *Issues of Sex Bias and Sex Fairness in Career Interest Measurement*, ed. E. E. Diamond, pp. 101-21. Washington, D.C.: U.S. Department of Health, Education, and Welfare.

——. 1974. "Interest Inventories: A Mixed Blessing." *Vocational Guidance Quarterly* (June): 280-86.

Birk, J. M., L. Barbanel, L. Brooks, M. H. Herman, J. B. Juhasz, R. A. Seltzer, and S. S. Tangri. 1974. "A Content Analysis of Sexual Bias in Commonly Used Psychology Textbooks." *Journal Supplement Abstract Service*, MS no. 733.

Birk, J. M., J. Cooper, and M. F. Tanney. 1975. "Stereotyping in Occupational Outlook Handbook Illustrations: A Follow-up Study." Paper presented to the American Psychological Association, Chicago.

——. 1973. "Racial and Sex Role Stereotyping in Career Illustrations." Paper presented at meeting of the American Psychological Association, Montreal.

Birk, J. M., and M. F. Tanney. 1972. *Career Exploration for High School Women: A Model*. Paper presented at the National Education Association Conference, November.

Bisconti, A. S. 1975. "College Graduates and their Employers—A National Study of Career Plans and Their Outcomes." *College Placement Council Foundation Report* (no. 4). Bethlehem, Pa.: CPC Foundation.

Bosmajian, H. A. 1972. "The Language of Sexism." *ETC: A Review of General Semantics* 29 (3): 305-13.

Boyer, E. 1973. *Women—Are the Technical-Occupational Programs Attracting Them?* Washington, D.C.: Women's Equity Action League Educational and Legal Defense Fund.

Brindley, F. B. 1971. "Social Factors Influencing Educational Aspiration of Black and White Girls." *Dissertation Abstracts International*. Ann Arbor, Mich.: University Microfilms, No. 71-1648.

Brooks, L. 1973. "Interactive Effects of Sex and Status on Self-disclosure." *Counseling Center Research Report* (no. 12-73). College Park, Md.: University of Maryland.

Broverman, I. K., D. M. Broverman, F. E. Clarkson, P. S. Rosenkrantz, and S. R. Vogel. 1970. "Sex-role Stereotypes and Clinical Judgements of Mental Health." *Journal of Consulting and Clinical Psychology* 34 (1): 1-7.

Brown, C. 1966. *Manchild in the Promised Land*. New York: New American Library, Inc.

Brown, C. R., and M. L. Hellinger. 1975. "Therapists' Attitudes toward Women." *Journal of Social Work* (July): 266-70.

Brown, M. D. 1974. "Sex Differences in Factors Affecting Educational Outcomes." Unpublished qualifying paper, Harvard University.

Campbell, D. P. 1973. "Women Deserve Better." *The Personnel and Guidance Journal* 51 (8): 545-49.

——. 1966. *Manual for the Strong Vocational Interest Blanks* (revised). Stanford, Calif.: Stanford University Press, 1966.

Campbell, M. A. 1973. *"Why Would a Girl Go into Medicine?"* Old Westbury, N.Y.: Feminist Press.

Campbell, P. B., and A. E. McKain. 1974. "Intellectual Decline and the Adolescent Woman." Paper presented at meeting of the American Psychological Association, Montreal.

Cannell, C. F., and R. L. Kahn. 1968. "Interviewing." In *The Handbook of Social Psychology*, ed. G. Lindzey and E. Aronson. Reading, Mass.: Addison-Wesley.

Carkhuff, R. R., and R. Pierce. 1967. "Differential Effects of Therapist Race and Social Class upon Patient Depth of Self-exploration in the Initial Interview." *Journal of Consulting Psychology* 31: 632-34.

Carnegie Commission on Higher Education (CCHE). 1968. *Quality and Equality: New Levels of Federal Responsibility for Higher Education*. Hightstown, N.J.: McGraw-Hill.

Carter, C. A. 1971. "Advantages of Being a Woman Therapist." *Psychotherapy: Theory, Research and Practice* 8 (4): 297–300.

Cartwright, D. S. 1955. "Success in Psychotherapy as a Function of Certain Actuarial Variables." *Journal of Consulting Psychology* 19: 357–63.

Centra, J. A. 1974. *Women, Men, and the Doctorate*. Princeton, N.J.: Educational Testing Service.

Christensen, K. C., and T. M. Magoon. 1974. "Perceived Hierarchy of Help-giving Sources for Two Categories of Student Problems." *Journal of Counseling Psychology* 21 (4): 311–14.

Christensen, K. C., and W. E. Sedlacek. 1972. "Differential Faculty Attitudes toward Blacks, Females and Students in General." *Counseling Center Research Report* (No. 13-72). College Park, Md.: University of Maryland.

Christensen, S., J. Melder, and B. A. Weisbrod. 1972. *Factors Affecting College Attendance*. Madison, Wis.: University of Wisconsin, Institute for Research on Poverty.

Chronicle of Higher Education. 1975. "20-Year Trends in Higher Education." 15 (Sept. 2).

Cohen, M. B. 1966. "Personal Identity and Sexual Identity." *Psychiatry* 29 (1): 1–14.

Cole, N. S. 1972. "On Measuring Vocational Interests of Women." *ACT Research Report* 49.

College Entrance Examination Board (CEEB). 1971a. *Barriers to Higher Education*. New York: CEEB.

———. 1971b. *Comparative Guidance and Placement Program*. Princeton, N.J.: CEEB.

Collins, A. M., and W. E. Sedlacek. 1974. "Counselor Ratings of Male and Female Clients." *Journal of National Association of Women Deans, Administrators and Counselors* 37 (3): 128–32.

Committee to Eliminate Sex Discrimination in the Public Schools and the Discrimination in Education Committee of NOW (Ann Arbor Chapter). 1972. *An Action Proposal to Eliminate Sex Discrimination in the Ann Arbor Public Schools*. Pittsburgh: KNOW, Inc.

Connell, D. M., and J. E. Johnson. 1970. "Relationship between Sex-role Identification and Self-esteem in Early Adolescents." *Developmental Psychology* 3 (2): 268.

Crandall, V., R. Dewey, W. Katkovsky, and A. Preston. 1964. "Parents' Attitudes and Behaviors and Grade-school Children's Academic Achievements." *Journal of Genetic Psychology* 104: 53–66.

Creager, J. A., A. W. Astin, R. F. Boruch, and A. E. Bayer. 1968. "National Norms for Entering College Freshmen–Fall 1968." *ACE Research Reports* 3 (1).

D'Costa, A. G. 1969. "The Role of Interests and Interest Measurement in Guidance." Paper presented at meeting of the American Personnel and Guidance Association, Las Vegas, Nev.

Dewey, C. R. 1974. "Exploring Interests: A Non-sexist Method." *The Personnel and Guidance Journal* 52 (5): 311-15.

Dickerson, K. G. 1974. "Are Female College Students Influenced by the Expectations They Perceive Their Faculty and Administration Have for Them?" *Journal of National Association of Women Deans, Administrators and Counselors* 37 (4): 167-72.

Doherty, M. A. 1973. "Sexual Bias in Personality Theory." *The Counseling Psychologist* 4 (1): 67-75.

Dorn, D. S. 1970. "Idealized Sex Roles among Young People." *Journal of Human Relations* 18 (1): 789-97.

El-Khawas, E. H., and A. S. Bisconti. 1974. *Five and Ten Years After College Entry*. Washington, D.C.: ACE.

Elman, J., A. Press, and P. Rosenkrantz. 1970. "Sex-Role Self-Concepts: Real and Ideal." Paper presented at annual meeting of the American Psychological Association, Miami Beach, Fla.

Entwisle, D. R., and E. Greenberger. 1972. "Adolescents' Views of Women's Work Role." *American Journal of Orthopsychiatry* 42 (4): 648-56.

Esterson, A., D. G. Cooper, and R. D. Laing. 1965. "Results of Family-Oriented Therapy with Hospitalized Schizophrenics." *British Medical Journal* 2: 1462-65.

Ewing, T. N. 1974. "Racial Similarity of Client and Counselor and Client Satisfaction with Counseling." *Journal of Counseling Psychology* 21 (5): 446-49.

Farmer, H. S., and M. J. Bohn, Jr. 1970. "Home-Career Conflict Reduction and the Level of Career Interest in Women." *Journal of Counseling Psychology* 17: 228-32.

Feather, N. T., and J. G. Simon. 1975. "Reactions to Male and Female Success and Failure in Sex-linked Occupations: Impressions of Personality, Causal Attributions, and Perceived Likelihood of Different Consequences." *Journal of Personality and Social Psychology* 31 (1): 20-31.

Fetters, W. B. 1975. *Student Questionnaire and Test Results by Sex, High School Program, Ethnic Category, and Father's Education, National Longitudinal Study of High School Class of 1972*. Washington, D.C.: U.S. Government Printing Office.

Flanagan, J. C., F. B. Davis, J. T. Dailey, M. F. Shaycoft, D. B. Orr, F. Goldberg, and C. A. Neyman, Jr. 1964. *Project TALENT: The American High-School Student*. Pittsburgh: University of Pittsburgh.

——. 1971. *Project TALENT: Five Years After High School*. Palo Alto, Calif.: American Institutes for Research; Pittsburgh: University of Pittsburgh.

Folger, J. K., H. S. Astin, and A. E. Bayer. 1970. *Human Resources and Higher Education*. New York: Russell Sage Foundation.

Frazier, N., and M. Sadker. 1973. *Sexism in School and Society*. New York: Harper and Row.

Friedersdorf, W. W. 1970. "A Comparative Study of Counselor Attitudes toward the Further Educational and Vocational Plans of High School Girls." *Dissertation Abstracts International* 30 (10): 4220-21.

Friedman, J. H. 1950. "Short-term Psychotherapy of 'Phobia of Travel'." *American Journal of Psychotherapy* 4: 259-78.

Friedman, N., L. W. Sanders, and J. Thompson. 1975. "Sex Discrimination in CWS?" *The Federal College Work Study Program: A Status Report, Fiscal Year 1971*. Washington, D.C.: U.S. Department of Health, Education, and Welfare, pp. 155-62.

Friedrich, L. K., and A. H. Stein. 1973. "Aggressive and Prosocial Television Programs and the Natural Behavior of Preschool Children." *Monograph of the Society for Research in Child Development* 38 (4).

Frieze, L. H., J. Fisher, M. C. McHugh, and V. A. Valle. 1975. "Attributing the Causes of Success and Failure: Internal and External Barriers to Achievement in Women." Draft of paper for conference on New Directions for Research on Women, Madison, Wisconsin, May 30–June 2.

Gardner, W. E. 1972. "The Differential Effects of Race, Education and Experience in Helping." *Journal of Clinical Psychology* 28: 87-89.

Garman, L. G., and W. T. Platt. 1974. "Sex Role Stereotypes and Educators' Descriptions of Mature Personalities." Paper presented at meeting of the Western Psychological Association, San Francisco, April.

Gazda, G. M. 1971. *Group Counseling: A Developmental Approach*. Boston: Allyn and Bacon.

Goldberg, P. 1968. "Are Women Prejudiced against Women?" *Trans-Action* 5 (5): 28-30.

Gottfredson, G. D., and J. L. Holland. 1975. "Vocational Choices of Men and Women: A Comparison of Predictors from the Self-directed Search." *Journal of Counseling Psychology* 22 (1): 28-34.

Gottsegen, G. B., and M. G. Gottsegen. 1973. "Women and School Psychology." *The School Psychology Digest* 2 (3): 24-27.

Grant, W. V., and C. G. Lind. 1975. *Digest of Educational Statistics: 1974 Edition*. Washington, D.C.: U.S. Government Printing Office.

Gump, J. P., and L. W. Rivers. 1975. "The Consideration of Race in Efforts to End Sex Bias." In *Issues of Sex Bias and Sex Fairness in Career Interest Measurement*, ed. E. E. Diamond, pp. 123-39. Washington, D.C.: U.S. Department of Health, Education, and Welfare.

Hansen, L. S. 1972. "We Are Furious (Female) but We Can Shape our Own Development." *Personnel and Guidance Journal* 51 (2): 87-93.

Hare, M. K. 1966. "Shortened Treatment in a Child Guidance Clinic: The Results in 119 Cases." *British Journal of Psychiatry* 112: 613-16.

Harmon, L. A. 1972. *Status of Women in Higher Education, 1963-1972: A Selected Bibliography*. Ames, Iowa: Iowa State University Library.

Harmon, L. W. 1971. "The Childhood and Adolescent Career Plans of College Women." *Journal of Vocational Behavior* 1 (1): 45-56.

——. 1970. "Strong Vocational Interest Blank Profiles of Disadvantaged Women." *Journal of Counseling Psuchology* 17 (6): 519-21.

Harrison, B. G. 1973. *Unlearning the Lie: Sexism in School*. New York: William Morrow.

Haun, L. E. 1974. "A Study of U.S. Counselor Educators by Sex." In *The Commission for Women 1973-1974 Report Summary*, pp. 4-6. Washington, D.C.: APGA.

Hawley, P. 1972. "Perceptions of Male Models of Femininity Related to Career Choice." *Journal of Counseling Psychology* 19 (4): 308-13.

——. 1971. "What Women Think Men Think: Does It Affect Their Career Choice?" *Journal of Counseling Psychology* 18 (3): 193-99.

Heffernon, A., and D. Bruehl. 1971. "Some Effects of Race of Inexperienced Lay Counselors on Black Jr. High School Students." *Journal of School Psychology* 9: 35-37.

Heilbrun, A. B., Jr. 1971. "Female Preference for Therapist Initial Interview Style as a Function of Client and Therapist Social Role Variables." *Journal of Counseling Psychology* 18 (4): 285-91.

——. 1969. "Parental Identification and the Patterning of Vocational Interests in College Males and Females." *Journal of Counseling Psychology* 16 (4): 342-47.

Hess, R. A. 1970. "Social Class and Ethnic Influences on Socialization." In *Carmichael's Manual of Child Psychology*, ed. P. H. Mussen, vol. 2, pp. 457-558. New York: John Wiley.

Hill, C. E. 1975. "Sex of Client and Sex and Experience Level of Counselor." *Journal of Counseling Psychology* 22 (1): 6-11.

Hill, C., M. Tanney, M. Leonard, and J. Reiss. 1977. "Reaction to Female Clients." *Journal of Counseling Psychology* 24 (1): 60-65.

Hishiki, P. C. 1969. "Self-concepts of Sixth Grade Girls of Mexican-American Descent." *California Journal of Educational Research* 20 (2): 56-62.

Hoffman, L. W. 1972. "Early Childhood Experiences and Women's Achievement Motives." *Journal of Social Issues* 28 (2): 129-55.

Holland, J. L. 1974. "Some Guidelines for Reducing Systematic Biases in the Delivery of Vocational Services." *Measurement and Evaluation in Guidance* 6: 210–18.

Hollender, J. 1972. "Sex Differences in Sources of Social Self-esteem." *Journal of Consulting and Clinical Psychology* 38 (3): 343–47.

Hollis, J. W., and R. A. Wantz. 1974. *Counselor Education Directory, 1974: Personnel and Programs*. Muncie, Ind.: Accelerated Development, Inc., Publication Division.

Holmstrom, E. I. 1975. "The New Pioneers: Women Engineering Students." Paper presented at Cornell University College of Engineering Conference, Ithaca, N.Y., June 24–27.

Horner, M. S. 1972. "Toward an Understanding of Achievement-related Conflicts in Women." *Journal of Social Issues* 28 (2): 157–75.

Howard, S. 1975. *Liberating Our Children, Ourselves*. Washington, D.C.: American Association of University Women.

Huth, C. M. 1973. "Measuring Women's Interests: How Useful?" *The Personnel and Guidance Journal* 51 (8): 539–45.

Iglitzen, L. B. 1973. "A Child's Eye View of Sex Roles." In *Sex-Role Stereotyping in the Schools*, pp. 23–30. Washington, D.C.: NEA.

Jencks, C., M. Smith, H. Acland, M. J. Bane, D. Cohen, H. Gintis, B. Heyns, and S. Mitchelson. 1972. *Inequality: A Reassessment of the Effect of Family and Schooling in America*. New York: Basic Books.

Johansson, C. B. 1975. "Technical Aspects: Problems of Scale Development, Norms, Item Differences by Sex and the Rate of Change in Occupational Group Characteristics." In *Issues of Sex Bias and Sex Fairness in Career Interest Measurement*, ed. E. E. Diamond, pp. 65–88. Washington, D.C.: U.S. Department of Health, Education, and Welfare.

Johansson, C. B., and L. W. Harmon. 1972. "Strong Vocational Interest Blank: One Form or Two?" *Journal of Counseling Psychology* 19 (5): 404–10.

Johnson, H. S. 1970. "Motivation and the Mexican-American." In *Educating the Mexican-American*, ed. H. S. Johnson and W. J. Hernandez, pp. 108–16. Valley Forge, Pa.: Judson Press.

Jones, H. 1973. *The Effects of Pre-College Counseling on the Educational and Career Aspirations of Blacks and Women Enrolled at the University of Pittsburgh*. Pittsburgh: University of Pittsburgh.

Kaplan, R. M., and R. D. Goldman. 1973. "Stereotypes of College Students toward the Average Man's and Woman's Attitudes toward Women." *Journal of Counseling Psychology* 20 (5): 459–62.

Klein, M. H. 1975. "Feminists' Concepts of Therapy Outcome." *Psychotherapy: Theory, Research, and Practice*.

Komarovsky, M. 1964. *Blue Collar Marriage*. New York: Random House.

Ladner, J. A. 1971. *Tomorrow's Tomorrow: The Black Woman.* Garden City, N.Y.: Doubleday.

Lasser, B. R. 1975. "An Outcomes-based Approach to Counseling Evaluation." *Measurement and Evaluation in Guidance* 8 (3): 136–44.

Laws, J. L. 1975. "Work Aspirations in Women: False Leads and New Starts." Draft prepared for Workshop Conference on Occupational Segregation, Wellesley, Mass.

Lazarus, A. A. 1963. "The Results of Behavior Therapy in 126 Cases of Severe Neurosis." *Behavior Research & Therapy* 1: 69–79.

Lerner, G., ed. 1973. *Black Women in White America. A Documentary History.* New York: Vintage Books.

Levy, B. 1973. "Sex-role Socialization in School." In *Sex-Role Stereotyping in the Schools,* pp. 1–7. Washington, D.C.: NEA.

Lewis, M. 1972. "Parents and Children: Sex-role Development." *The School Review* 80 (2): 229–40.

Liebert, R. M., J. M. Neale, and E. S. Davidson. 1973. *The Early Window: Effects of Television on Children and Youth.* New York: Pergamon Press.

Los Angeles Unified School District. 1975. *Follow up Study of Los Angeles City 1973 High School Graduates One Year After Graduation,* Report 346. Los Angeles: Unified School District, Research and Evaluation Branch.

Luff, M. C., and M. Garrod. 1935. "The After-results of Psychotherapy in 500 Adult Cases." *British Medical Journal* 2: 54–59.

Lunneborg, P. W., and C. Lillie. 1973. "Sexism in Graduate Admissions." *American Psychologist* (Feb.): 197–89.

Lyle, J., and Hoffman, H. R. 1972. "Children's Use of Television and Other Media." In *Television and Social Behavior,* ed. E. A. Rubinstein, G. A. Comstock, and J. P. Murray. Reports and Papers IV: Television in Day-to-Day Life: Patterns of Use, pp. 129–256. Washington, D.C.: U.S. Government Printing Office.

Maccoby, E. E., and Jacklin, C. N. 1974. *The Psychology of Sex Differences.* Stanford, Calif.: Stanford University Press.

Mackeen, B. A., and A. Herman. 1974. "Effects of Group Counseling on Self-esteem." *Journal of Counseling Psychology* 21 (3): 210–14.

MacLeod, J. S., and S. T. Silverman. 1973. *You Won't Do.* Pittsburgh: KNOW, Inc.

Maslin, A., and J. L. Davis. 1975. "Sex-role Stereotyping as a Factor in Mental Health Standards among Counselors-in-Training." *Journal of Counseling Psychology* 22 (2): 87–91.

McCandless, B. R. 1969. "Childhood Socialization." In *Handbook of Socialization Theory and Research*, ed. D. A. Goslin, pp. 791–819. Chicago: Rand McNally.

McClelland, D. C., J. R. Atkinson, R. A. Clark, and E. L. Lowell. 1953. *The Achievement Motive*. New York: Appleton-Century-Crofts.

Melnick, R. R. 1975. "Counseling Response as a Function of Problem Presentation and Type of Problem." *Journal of Counseling Psychology* 22: 6–11.

Meltzoff, J., and M. Kornreich. 1970. *Research in Psychotherapy*. New York: Atherton.

Mezzano, J. 1971. "Concerns of Students and Preference for Male and Female Counselors." *Vocational Guidance Quarterly* 20 (1): 42–47.

Mischel, W. 1970. "Sex-typing and Socialization." In *Carmichael's Manual of Child Psychology*, ed. P. H. Mussen, vol. 2, pp. 3–72. New York: John Wiley.

Mitchell, J. 1974. *Psychoanalysis and Feminism*. New York: Vintage.

Mitchell, J. S. 1975. *I Can Be Anything: Careers and Colleges for Young Women*. New York: CEEB.

Mowsesian, R. 1972. "Educational and Career Aspirations of High School Females." *Journal of National Association of Women Deans and Counselors* 35 (2): 65–70.

National Institute of Education (NIE) Career Education Staff. 1975. "Guideline for Assessment of Sex Bias and Sex Fairness in Career Interest Inventories." In *Issues of Sex Bias and Sex Fairness in Career Interest Measurement*, ed. E. E. Diamond, pp. xxiii–xxix. Washington, D.C.: U.S. Department of Health, Education, and Welfare. (Available from Educational Work, NIE, Washington, D.C. 20208.)

National Institutes of Health (NIH). 1968. *Special Report on Women and Graduate Study in the United States*. Resources for Medical Research Report 13. Washington, D.C.: U.S. Department of Health, Education, and Welfare, NIH.

National Scholarship Service and Fund for Negro Students (NSSFNS). 1972. "A National Profile of Black Youth: The Class of 1971." *NSSFNS Research Reports* 1 (1).

Padilla, M., and P. Aranda. 1974. *Latino Mental Health*. Washington, D.C.: U.S. Government Printing Office.

Peoples, V. Y., and D. M. Dell. 1975. "Black and White Student Preferences for Counselor Roles." *Journal of Counseling Psychology* 22 (6): 529–34.

Perez, M. S. 1975. "Counseling Services at UCSC: Attitudes and Perspectives of Chicano Students." Unpublished manuscript, Santa Cruz, Calif.

Pettigrew, H. F. 1964. *A Profile of the Negro American*. Princeton, N.J.: Van Noss.

Phelps, A. T., H. S. Farmer, and T. E. Backer. 1976. *Bibliography on Women at Work*. New York: Human Science Press.

Pine, G. J. 1975. "Evaluating School Guidance Programs: Retrospect and Prospect." *Measurement and Evaluation in Guidance* 8 (3): 136-44.

Plost, R. 1976. "Career Media Centers Are Short Changing Today's Girls." Cited in Phelps, Farmer, and Backer, *Bibliography on Women at Work*, q.v.

Prediger, D. J. 1972. "Tests and Developmental Career Guidance: The Untried Relationship." *Measurement and Evaluation in Guidance* 5: 426-29.

Pressley, B. O. 1974. "Survey of Guidance and Counseling Divisions of State Departments of Education." *The Commission for Women 1973-1974 Report Summary*, p. 3. Washington, D.C.: APGA.

Putnam, B. A., and J. G. Hansen. 1972. "Relationship of Self-concept and Feminine Role Concept to Vocational Maturity in Young Women." *Journal of Counseling Psychology* 19 (5): 436-40.

Rachman, S. 1963. "Studies in Desensitization: I. The Separate Effects of Relaxation and Desensitization." *Behavior Research & Therapy* 1: 133-37.

Rennie, S., and K. Grimstad, eds. 1975. *New Woman's Survival Sourcebook*. New York: Knopf.

Resource Center on Sex Roles. 1974. *Today's Changing Roles: An Approach to Non-Sexist Teaching*. Washington, D.C.: NEA.

Roby, P. 1973. "Institutional Barriers to Women Students in Higher Education." In *Academic Women on the Move*, ed. A. S. Rossi and A. Calderwood, pp. 37-56. New York: Russell Sage Foundation.

Rodriguez, A., M. Rodriguez, and L. Eisenberg. 1959. "The Outcome of School Phobia: A Following Study Based on 41 Cases." *American Journal of Psychiatry* 116: 540-44.

Rogers, C. R., and R. F. Dymond, eds. *Psychotherapy and Personality Change*. Chicago: University of Chicago Press, 215-37.

Rosenkrantz, P., S. Vogel, H. Bee, D. M. Broverman, and I. Broverman. 1968. "Sex-role Stereotypes and Self-concepts in College Students." *Journal of Consulting and Clinical Psychology* 32 (3): 287-95.

Rosenthal, D., and T. D. Frank. 1958. "The Fate of Psychiatric Clinic Outpatients Assigned to Psychotherapy." *Journal of Nervous Mental Disease* 127: 330-43.

Rosenthal, R., and L. Jacobson. 1968. *Pygmalion in the Classroom*. New York: Holt, Rinehart and Winston.

Saario, T. N., C. N. Jacklin, and C. K. Tittle. 1973. "Sex Role Stereotyping in the Public Schools." *Harvard Educational Review* 43 (3): 386-416.

Scher, M. 1975. "Verbal Activity, Sex, Counselor Experience and Success in Counseling." *Journal of Counseling Psychology* 22 (2): 97-101.

Schlossberg, N. K. 1974. "Liberated Counseling: A Question Mark." *Journal of the National Association of Women Deans, Administrators, and Counselors* 38 (1): 3-10.

Schlossberg, N. K., and J. Goodman. 1972a. "A Woman's Place: Children's Sex Stereotyping of Occupations." *Vocational Guidance Quarterly* 20 (4): 266-70.

———. 1972b. "Imperative for Change: Counselor Use of the Strong Vocational Interest Blanks." *Impact* 2 (1): 25-29.

Schlossberg, N. K., and J. J. Pietrofesa. 1974. "Perspectives on Counselors Bias: Implications for Counselor Education." *The Counseling Psychologist* 4 (1): 44-54.

Schmidt, E., D. Castell, and P. Brown. 1965. "A Retrospective Study of 72 Cases of Behavior Therapy." *Behavior Research & Therapy* 3: 9-19.

Schneider, J. W., and S. L. Hacker. 1973. "Sex Role Imagery and Use of the Generic 'Man' in Introductory Texts: A Case in the Sociology of Sociology." *The American Sociologist* 8: 12-18.

Schramm, W., J. Lyle, and E. B. Parker. 1961. *Television in the Lives of Our Children.* Stanford, Calif.: Stanford University Press.

Sears, P. S., and D. H. Feldman. 1966. "Teacher Interactions with Boys and with Girls." *The National Elementary Principal* 46 (2): 30-35.

Seifer, N. 1973. *Absent From the Majority: Working Class Women in America.* New York: Institute of Human Relations.

Sewell, W. H., and R. M. Hauser. 1975. *Education, Occupation, and Earnings: Achievement in the Early Career.* New York: Academic Press.

Sewell, W. H., and V. P. Shah. 1967. "Socioeconomic Status, Intelligence, and the Attainment of Higher Education." *Sociology of Education* 40 (1): 1-23.

Sharp, W. H., and B. A. Kirk. 1974. "A Longitudinal Study of Who Seeks Counseling When." *Journal of Counseling Psychology* 21 (1): 43-50.

Shaw, M. C., and D. L. White. 1965. "The Relationship between Child Parent Identification and Academic Underachievement." *Journal of Clinical Psychology* 21: 10-13.

Shepard, W. O., and D. T. Hess. 1975. "Attitudes in Four Age Groups Toward Sex-role Division in Adult Occupations and Activities." *Journal of Vocational Behavior* 6 (1): 27-39.

Shertzer, B., and S. C. Stone. 1971. *Fundamentals of Guidance.* 2d ed. New York: Houghton Mifflin.

Simon, K. A., and M. M. Frankel. 1975. *Projections of Educational Statistics to 1983-84: 1974 Edition.* Washington, D.C.: U.S. Government Printing Office.

Smith, M. L. 1974. "Influence of Client Sex and Ethnic Group on Counselor Judgements." *Journal of Counseling Psychology* 21: 516-21.

Sobel, R. 1962. "The Private Practice of Child Psychiatry. A Ten-year Study." *American Journal of Psychotherapy* 16: 567-79.

State of North Carolina, Department of Public Instruction. N.d. *Elimination of Traditional Sex Stereotypes in Public Schools, Suggested Directions and Strategies.* Raleigh, N.C.: State Department of Instruction.

Stein, A. H., and M. M. Bailey. 1973. "The Socialization of Achievement Orientation in Females." *Psychological Bulletin* 80 (5): 345-66.

Stein, A. H., and J. Smithells. 1969. "Age and Sex Differences in Children's Sex-role Standards about Achievement." *Developmental Psychology* 1 (3): 252-59.

Steinmann, A. 1970. "Female-role Perception as a Factor in Counseling." *Journal of the National Association of Women Deans and Counselors* (fall): 27-32.

——. 1963. "A Study of the Concept of the Feminine Role of 51 Middle-class American Families." *Genetic Psychology Monographs* 67: 275-352.

——. 1959. "Women's Attitudes towards Careers." *Vocational Guidance Quarterly* (autumn): 15-18.

Steinmann, A., and D. J. Fox. 1966. "Male Female Perceptions of the Female Role in the United States." *Journal of Psychology* 64: 265-76.

Sue, D. W., and B. A. Kirk. 1975. "Asian Americans: Use of Counseling and Psychiatric Services on a College Campus." *Journal of Counseling Psychology* 22 (1): 84-86.

Sue, S., and H. L. Kitano. 1973. "Stereotypes as a Measure of Success." *The Journal of Social Issues* 29 (2): 83-98.

Tanney, M. F. 1975. "Face Validity of Interest Measures: Sex-role Stereotyping." In *Issues of Sex Bias and Sex Fairness in Career Interest Measurement*, ed. E. E. Diamond, pp. 89-99. Washington, D.C.: Department of Health, Education, and Welfare.

Task Force on the Status of Women in Psychology (TFSWP). 1972. *Survey of Departments of Psychology.* Washington, D.C.: APA.

Thomas, A. H., and N. R. Stewart. 1971. "Counselor Response to Female Clients with Deviate and Conforming Career Goals." *Journal of Counseling Psychology* 18 (4): 352-57.

Thompson, B. W. 1974. *Tabular Summary of Student Questionnaire Data, National Longitudinal Study of the High School Class of 1972*, vols. 1 and 2. Washington, D.C.: U.S. Government Printing Office.

Thorndike, R. L., ed. 1971. *Educational Measurement.* Washington, D.C.: ACE.

Thorndike, R. L., and E. Hagen. 1971. *Measurement and Evaluation in Psychology and Education.* 3d ed. New York: John Wiley.

Tiedt, I. M. 1972. "Realistic Counseling for High School Girls." *The School Counselor* 19 (5): 354–56.

Tittle, C. K., K. McCarthy, and J. F. Steckler. 1974. *Women and Educational Testing.* Princeton, N.J.: Educational Testing Service.

Turner, B. F., and J. H. McCaffery. 1974. "Socialization and a Career Orientation among Black and White College Women." *Journal of Vocational Behavior* 5 (3): 307–19.

Turner, B. F., and C. Turner. 1974. *Race and Sex Differences in Evaluating Women.* Paper presented at meeting the American Psychological Association, New Orleans.

Tyler, L. 1971. *Tests and Measurements.* 2d ed. Englewood Cliffs, N.J.: Prentice-Hall.

———. 1969. *The Work of the Counselor.* 3d ed. New York: Appleton-Century-Crofts.

U.S. Bureau of the Census. 1975a. *Characteristics of American Youth: 1974.* Current Population Reports, Special Studies, Series P-23 (51). Washington, D.C.: U.S. Government Printing Office.

———. 1975b. *Income and Expenses of Students Enrolled in Postsecondary Schools: October, 1973.* Current Population Reports, Special Studies, Series P-20 (281). Washington, D.C.: U.S. Government Printing Office.

U.S. Department of Health, Education, and Welfare, National Center for Educational Statistics. 1974. *National Longitudinal Study of the High School Class of 1972.* Washington, D.C.: U.S. Government Printing Office.

U.S. Department of Labor, Bureau of Labor Statistics. 1972. *Occupational Outlook Handbook, 1972.* Washington, D.C.: U.S. Government Printing Office.

———. 1974. *Occupational Outlook Handbook, 1974.* Washington, D.C.: U.S. Government Printing Office.

U.S. Office of Education. 1976. *Equality of Educational Opportunity.* Washington, D.C.: U.S. Government Printing Office.

University of California, Los Angeles, University Extension. 1974. *Sounds of Change: A Report on Training in Counseling and Programming for Women's Career Opportunities.* Los Angeles: UCLA Extension.

Vener, A. M., and C. A. Snyder. 1966. "The Preschool Child's Awareness and Anticipation of Adult Sex-roles." *Sociometry* 29: 159–68.

Vetter, L. 1975. "Sex Stereotyping in Illustrations in Career Materials." Paper presented at meeting of the American Psychological Association, Chicago, September.

Vogel, S. R., I. K. Broverman, D. M. Broverman, F. E. Clarkson, and P. S. Rosenkrantz. 1970. "Maternal Employment and Perception of Sex Roles among College Students." *Developmental Psychology* 3 (3): 384–91.

Walster, E., T. A. Cleary, and M. M. Clifford. 1970. "The Effect of Race and Sex on College Admission." *Sociology of Education* 44 (spring): 237-44.

Warren, W. 1965. "A Study of Adolescent Psychiatric In-patients and the Outcome Six or More Years Later: II. The Follow-up Study." *Journal of Child Psychology and Psychiatry* 6: 141-60.

Watley, D. J. 1971. "Bright Black Youth: Their Educational Plans and Career Aspirations." National Merit Scholarship Corporation Research Report 7 (8).

Weisstein, N. 1971. "Psychology Constructs the Female." In *Women in Sexist Society: Studies in Power and Powerlessness*, ed. V. Gornick and B. K. Boran, pp. 207-24. New York: Basic Books.

Weitzman, L. J., D. Eifler, E. Hokada, and C. Ross. 1972. "Sex Role Socialization in Picture Books for Preschool Children." *American Journal of Sociology* 77 (6): 1125-50.

Werts, C. E. 1960. "A Comparison of Male vs. Female College Attendance Probabilities." *Sociology of Education* 41 (1): 103-20.

Westervelt, E. M. 1975. *Barriers to Women's Participation in Postsecondary Education.* Washington, D.C.: U.S. Government Printing Office.

———. 1973. "A Tide in the Affairs of Women: The Psychological Impact of Feminism on Educated Women." *The Counseling Psychologist* 4 (1): 3-26.

Westervelt, E. M., and D. A. Fixter. 1971. *Women's Higher and Continuing Education: An Annotated Bibliography with Selected References on Related Aspects of Women's Lives.* New York: CEEB.

Whiteley, J. 1975. *Guidance Theories.* Unpublished manuscript.

Whiteley, R. 1975. *Assertion Training for Women.* Unpublished manuscript.

———. 1973. "Women in groups." *The Counseling Psychologist* 4 (1): 27-43.

Whitfield, E. A., and A. Gustav, eds. 1972. *Counseling Girls and Women Over the Life Span.* Washington, D.C.: APGA, National Vocational Guidance Association.

Whitton, M. C. 1975. "Same-sex and Cross-sex Reliability and Concurrent Validity of the Strong-Campbell Interest Inventory." *Journal of Counseling Psychology* 22 (3): 204-90.

Wilms, W. W. 1974. *Public and Proprietary Vocational Training: A Study of Effectiveness.* Berkeley, Calif.: University of California, Berkeley, Center for Research in Higher Education.

Women on Words and Images. 1975. *Channeling Children, Sex Stereotyping in Prime-Time TV.* Princeton, N.J.: Women on Words and Images.

———. 1972. *Dick and Jane as Victims.* Princeton, N.J.: Women on Words and Images.

Woellner, E. H. 1974. *Requirements for Certification for Elementary Schools, Secondary Schools, Junior Colleges*. Chicago: University of Chicago Press.

Wren, S. C. 1975. *The College Student and Higher Education Policy*. Berkeley, Calif.: The Carnegie Foundation for the Advancement of Teaching.

Wright, R. 1937. *Black Boy*. New York: Harper.

Wyckoff, H. 1974a. "Banal Script of Women." In *Scripts People Live*, ed. C. Steiner, pp. 175–96. New York: Grove Press.

———. 1974b. "Sex Role Scripting in Men and Women." In *Scripts People Live*, ed. C. Steiner, pp. 165–75. New York: Grove Press.

Zigler, E., and I. L. Child. 1968. "Socialization." In *The Handbook of Social Psychology*, vol. 3, ed. G. Lindzey and E. Aronson, pp. 450–589. Reading Mass.: Addison-Wesley.

Zytowski, D. G. 1969. "Toward a Theory of Career Development for Women." *Personnel and Guidance Journal* 47: 660–64.

ABOUT THE AUTHORS

MICHELE HARWAY is a research psychologist at the Higher Education Research Institute. Previously, she was Director of Women's Programs and Assistant Dean of Students at the University of California, Irvine.

For the past six years, Dr. Harway has been conducting research on the college environment and on student development with an emphasis on attitudes toward women and women's career development. She is the author of more than a dozen articles in such professional journals as the *Journal of College Student Personnel*, the *Psychology of Women Quarterly*, the *College Student Journal*, and the *Journal of the National Association of Women Deans, Administrators and Counselors*. She has coauthored a chapter on counseling and student development in the *Annual Review of Psychology*.

In addition to her research interests, Michele Harway was involved in developing women's studies and in doing assertion training for women at the University of Maryland. More recently she has done crisis intervention counseling and training. She has served on the Board of Directors of the Los Angeles Commission on Assaults Against Women and is an associate of the Counseling Center, University of Maryland.

HELEN S. ASTIN is Professor of Higher Education at the Graduate School of Education at UCLA, and Vice-President of the Higher Education Research Institute. Previously, she was Director of Research and Education for the University Research Corporation in Washington, D.C. Her research interests are in the fields of educational progress and career development with an emphasis on women.

Dr. Astin has been Chairperson of the American Psychological Association's Task Force on the Status of Women in Psychology and President of Division 35 (Division of the Psychology of Women) of the American Psychological Association. Currently she is serving on the association's Board for Policy and Planning. She is a member of the National Research Council Board on Human-Resource Data and Analyses and a Trustee of Hampshire College. She serves on the Editorial Boards of the *Journal of Counseling Psychology, Journal of Vocational Behavior, Psychology of Women Quarterly, Signs*, and *Sage Annuals in Women's Policy Studies*.

Among Helen Astin's publications are: *Human Resources and Higher Education; The Woman Doctorate in America; Women: A Bibliography on Their Education and Careers; Higher Education and the Disadvantaged Student; Open Admissions at CUNY; Sex Roles: An Annotated Research Bibliography;* and *The Power of Protest.*